YIELD TO JESUS

YIELD TO JESUS

A DEVOTIONAL

Written and Edited by

BEVERLY COURREGE

A JANET THOMA BOOK

THOMAS NELSON PUBLISHERS
Nashville

Published in Nashville, Tennessee, by Thomas Nelson, Inc.

Unless otherwise noted, Scripture quotations are from THE NEW KING JAMES VERSION.
Copyright © 1979, 1980, 1982, Thomas Nelson, Inc., Publishers.

Scripture quotations noted The Message are from *The Message: The New Testament in Contemporary
English.* Copyright © 1993 by Eugene H. Peterson.

Scripture quotations noted NASB are from the NEW AMERICAN STANDARD BIBLE®,
© Copyright The Lockman Foundation 1960, 1962, 1963, 1968, 1971, 1972, 1973, 1975,
1977. Used by permission.

Scripture quotations noted NIV are from the HOLY BIBLE: NEW INTERNATIONAL VER-
SION®. Copyright © 1973, 1978, 1984 by International Bible Society. Used by permission
of Zondervan Publishing House. All rights reserved.

Scripture quotations noted NLT are from the *Holy Bible,* New Living Translation, copyright ©
1996. Used by permission of Tyndale House Publishers, Inc., Wheaton, Illinois 60189. All
rights reserved.

Library of Congress Cataloging-in-Publication Data

Y2J: yield to Jesus : a devotional / [compiled by] Beverly Courrege.
   p. cm.
  Includes bibliographical references.
  ISBN 0-7852-6852-9 (hc)
  1. Meditations. I. Courrege, Beverly. II. Title: Yield to Jesus.
BV4832.Y13 1999
242—dc21

99–39346
CIP

Printed in the United States of America
1 2 3 4 5 6 BVG 04 03 02 01 00 99

DEDICATION

Cassie of Columbine, you shall not be forgotten . . .

"Assuredly, I say to you, wherever this gospel is preached in the whole world, what this woman has done will also be told as a memorial to her."

Matthew 26:13

CONTENTS

Contents

Contents

ACKNOWLEDGMENTS

Blessings to you, Janet, my editor and my friend! Thank you for the privilege of working with you and your team on *Y2J*.

Special thanks to Anne Trudel, Managing Editor, Janet Thoma Books. I know there are some things you accomplished for this project that surely surpass your job description! Our daily visits via e-mail, fax, and phone will indeed be fond memories friend to friend!

To the Thomas Nelson authors who said "yes!" to *Y2J*, thank you. I know the readers of this book will be eternally blessed by your edifying words.

To my son, Cord. Without your faster-than-cyberspeed ability to transcribe selected works, 60,000 words times "three" (you had to be there), I would have been lost. Glad you were with me! Love, Mom

And to the other Courreges! Joe, Toni, Tracy, Angie, Kit and his bride, Lori . . . this special mention because of a printing omission in another book, never an intentional omission. Love, Beas

BREAK-IN, BREAKOUT!

A man can no more be a Christian without facing evil and conquering it, than he can be a soldier without going to battle, facing the cannon's mouth, and encountering the enemy in the field.

—E.H. Chapin (1814–80)
American clergyman

One weekend afternoon my infant daughter, J.J., was sleeping in her cradle near the bed where my two-year-old son, Cord, and I were napping. I had turned the television on low volume to cartoons in case Cord woke before I did.

Cord did wake me asking, "Mom, who is that man?" I was startled to see a grown man standing at the foot of my bed—between us and the cradle! He had a finger to his lips, signaling, "Hush!"

Terror rushed through me. I didn't scream because I didn't want Cord to start crying.

1

The man walked across the hall to the bathroom, still watching us. He came back into the bedroom and repeated the "Hush!" gesture. Then he walked down the hallway toward our kitchen and started going through the drawers. I panicked. Our only exits were the kitchen and the front door, which was adjacent to the kitchen.

Hurriedly, I grabbed the phone and called my brother-in-law, who lived nearby. In a screaming whisper, I told him there was a man in my duplex and asked him to call the police. Seconds later, he had the details and I hung up.

I could still hear the intruder. *What can I do?* I thought. I took J.J. from her crib and brought her in the bed with us. I held her in one arm and wrapped my other arm around Cord. Then I cried, "Lord, help me! I don't know what to do!"

Just a moment later, I noticed our ground-floor window for the first time. All I had to do was open the window, crawl through it with the kids, go out the backyard gate, and find someone at home in our neighborhood. Minutes later we were in the safe haven of a neighbor's home.

Meanwhile, the police arrived. My intruder turned out to be the twenty-seven-year-old autistic son of a neighbor's cleaning lady. He had found my front door unlocked and wandered into our house. When the police arrived, he was still in my kitchen, looking for something to eat.

As Christians, it is comforting to know that we have access *at all times* to the One who rescues us. When we yield our thoughts to God, we can face any evils with the confidence that He has plans for our well-being on His mind.

I have heard Jeremiah 33:3 referred to as "God's phone number."

It reads, "Call to Me, and I will answer you, and show you great and mighty things, which you do not know." On that day of our break-in, I am so thankful that God didn't have a busy signal, call waiting, or a "please hold" recording!

> For I know the thoughts that I think toward you, says the Lord, thoughts of peace and not of evil, to give you a future and a hope. Then you will call upon Me and go and pray to Me, and I will listen to you. And you will seek Me and find Me, when you search for Me with all your heart. I will be found by you, says the LORD, and I will bring you back from your captivity. (Jer. 29:11–14a)

READER'S NOTES:

_____

_____

_____

_____

_____

_____

A Map for All Time

The Bible is a map and a survival manual for the Christian life.

—Tim Hansel
Through the Wilderness of Loneliness[1]

I still remember a story I heard twenty years ago about my favorite Old Testament hero, Jonathan. The speaker compared Jonathan's tactics and leadership during battle to a British general during World War I.

First Viscount Edmund Henry Hynman Allenby (1861–1936) was appointed in 1917 to head the British and Commonwealth cavalries in Egypt and Palestine. In October 1917 General Allenby's troops took control of Beersheba, breaking through the Germans' line of defense. Then they vigorously pursued the retreating Turks, seized Jaffa, split the Turkish armies, turned inland, and took Jerusalem in December.

4

But Allenby's defining moment came in September. In just thirty-eight days he advanced his troops 350 miles, taking 72,000 Turkish and 4,000 German and Austrian prisoners, compared with his own losses of 5,600. Turkey finally surrendered.

The most incredible "God-incidence" in this story is the route on which General Allenby took his men. I remember the speaker saying General Allenby recalled reading in the Scriptures about Jonathan's battles in the same area that was called the Holy Land in 1918. Allenby first took Beersheba captive. So did Jonathan. Next Allenby took modern-day Jaffa. Jonathan chose to take Askelon and Gaza (near Jaffa on the coast) before sending an advance army to secure Jerusalem. While Jonathan sent his troops to Jerusalem, he went next to Damascus. Every strategic point that Jonathan secured was part of Allenby's route for his troops.

The final three cities that Allenby secured after Jerusalem were Megiddo, Damascus, and Aleppo. Jonathan captured Megiddo and Damascus, too, in the same order. Incidentally, Jonathan did not easily win the battle of Megiddo. Megiddo was a walled city on a mountain. It was taken by Joshua (Josh. 12:21), and the Israelites secured it for good during King Solomon's reign.

Too much information? Even if you are not a history buff, aren't you curious about the amazing parallel between Jonathan and General Allenby's forces? I believe Allenby followed Jonathan's pattern and, perhaps, his strategy for Megiddo. One account of the 1918 battle of Megiddo is described as "a *great* cavalry battle where Allenby routed the Egyptians."

Why does it matter to me? I think the final chapter of this story has not yet happened. Why do I say this? The "mountain of Megiddo" in Hebrew (Rev. 16:16) means *Armageddon*.

Forever, O Lord,
Your word is settled in heaven.
Your faithfulness endures to all generations;
You established the earth, and it abides.
They continue this day according to Your ordinances,
For all are Your servants.
Unless Your law had been my delight,
I would then have perished in my affliction.
I will never forget Your precepts,
For by them You have given me life. (Ps. 119:89–93)

READER'S NOTES:

_____
_____
_____
_____
_____
_____
_____

Y2J Yield to Jesus

CHARACTER, CONDUCT, AND CONVERSATION

BY CHARLES STANLEY

Y ou have no idea who is observing you nearby or from a distance. Sometimes people start out watching with curiosity. They watch to see if your faith really does work. It's a compliment to know that your life has stirred up interest in others. However, three essentials must be operative before you can expect anyone to check out your faith.

First, your character needs to be solid. What you are on the inside is so much more important than what you look like on the outside.

Before Philip went to the Ethiopian eunuch, he had already

exhibited a godly character. Philip was chosen because of his good reputation (Acts 6). He was humble in that he was willing to serve tables. He was sincere: "And the multitudes with one accord heeded the things spoken by Philip, hearing and seeing the miracles which he did" (Acts 8:6). The people gave him attention because they knew he was sincere. People can generally tell if a person is sincere. I call it feeling sick in my spirit when someone doesn't ring true when speaking.

Philip was obedient. He left an exciting ministry and a tremendous meeting to go to the desert. From my perspective as a preacher, I can only imagine what he was thinking. But he went. Read the description of the meeting: "For unclean spirits, crying with a loud voice, came out of many who were possessed; and many who were paralyzed and lame were healed. And there was great joy in that city" (Acts 8:7–8). All that was going on when an angel of the Lord met Philip and said—with apparently no explanation—"Arise and go toward the south" (Acts 8:26). The Bible adds that it was a desert road.

Can you imagine what it would be like for God to be using you in a great and mighty way and then tell you He needs you in an apparently desert-like experience? Well, Philip's character of obedience matched his humble spirit, and his servant's spirit and he "arose and went" (Acts 8:27).

Philip was a man of faith—he went without much instruction. He was zealous in spirit because the Bible says he ran after the chariot that he found in the desert. And he was courageous. Persecution was abounding in the church. Stephen had just been stoned. But Philip ran to give testimony to a man sitting in a chariot.

That's character.

The second essential that must be true before you can expect anyone to be curious about your life is conduct, or what you do. Philip was of a good reputation. He had been watched in the early church, and apparently, his conduct was excellent. He was one of seven men put in charge.

Conduct reveals character. When God said, "Preach to the multitudes, Philip," he preached to the multitudes (Acts 8:6). And when God said, "Preach to one, Philip," he ran to catch up with the one. He could have moaned, "Oh, God, come on. I don't want to go to just one. There's a lot going on with the multitudes. Please let me stay with the group." Apparently, no such conversation took place. Philip's conduct matched his character. He did what he was asked, no matter what the task.

What does your conduct say? No, not what do your lips say. What does your conduct say? Words come easily. A godly walk—or conduct—needs to be maintained and carefully watched over. Unbelievers have very high standards for you. They know you shouldn't listen to their jokes. They know you should be a faithful employee. They know your entertainment should be different than theirs.

Your conduct must match your character so that you may be an effective witness for the sake of the kingdom.

A third essential that must be true before you can expect anyone to be curious about your life is your conversation. Your conversation will either cloud or confirm your character and your conduct. When Philip ran after the man in the chariot on the desert road, the eunuch was reading out loud, which was customary in those days. Philip's conversation began, "Do you understand what you are reading?" (Acts 8:30). After the Ethiopian eunuch acknowledged he needed someone to help him understand the book of Isaiah, Philip jumped up and sat with him.

Notice that he didn't just jump in and take over before he was invited. He waited until he was invited into the chariot, saw what passage the man was reading, and "Philip opened his mouth, and beginning at this Scripture, preached Jesus to him" (Acts 8:35). Notice, he did not start from Genesis 1. He started where the man was and responded to the man's questions and showed him the Lord Jesus Christ.

That's what a testimony should be. Jesus should be the center of attention, not you.

After Philip's presentation of the gospel, the eunuch got excited and spotted some water in the desert. He immediately wanted to be baptized. Philip went over the gospel once more to make sure the man understood. Philip's conversation made the gospel crystal clear. Your testimony and mine can do the same thing.

Excerpted from *The Glorious Journey* by Charles Stanley (Nashville: Thomas Nelson, Inc., 1996), 453–454. Used by permission.

He has shown you, O man, what is good;
And what does the Lord require of you
But to do justly,
To love mercy,
And to walk humbly with your God? (Mic. 6:8)

11-18-02   Steven Curtis Chapman song

READER'S NOTES:
Character
Conduct
Conversation

Y2J Yield to Jesus

DID YOU SAY BRAIN TUMOR?

As honey to the mouth, as melody to the ear, as a song of gladness to the heart, is the Name of Jesus. But it is also a medicine.

—Saint Bernard (1091–1152)
French ecclesiastic

At 6:00 A.M. one January day in 1981, my husband, Boo, left for a sales convention in Atlanta. I was walking down the hallway of our home when my vision blurred, my tongue felt thick, and my hands and feet went numb, causing me to stagger shakily back to bed. I sank onto the mattress in a state of semi-consciousness.

At some point I realized I might not be able to get up. (My children had spent the night next door with their friends, so I was alone.) I called my sister-in-law mid-morning and asked her to take me to the emergency room, where I was met by my doctor and an elder from our church. By noon my brain waves and heartbeat were being monitored, and I was scheduled for more extensive testing throughout the day. My preliminary diagnosis was grim—my symptoms indicated that at best, I could end up paralyzed, and at worst, I could die within forty-eight hours.

My sister-in-law and our church elder remained by my side, constantly comforting me and praying for me. They reached Boo in Atlanta, and by 10:00 P.M. he was at my side to "join the watch."

The next morning, another test revealed that I had a brain tumor. The doctors told my husband about the tumor that afternoon and said it would be the next day before they could tell whether the tumor was active (malignant) or benign. My husband and friends decided to spare me the anguish of this new development. While I slept peacefully, unaware of this new crisis, members of my church and many other intercessors were praying on my behalf.

The second test revealed that my tumor was inactive; it was "calcified." Forty-eight hours after I was admitted to the hospital with a life-threatening diagnosis, my symptoms were diminishing, some even having disappeared completely.

My third morning in the hospital, a friend brought a tray of food in to me. Scripture verses were taped to each corner of the tray. I later learned that the tray belonged to another dear sister in the Lord who went home to be with Him after her illness with a brain tumor.

Ironically, the friend who had brought in my food tray went home to be with the Lord fifteen years later. Her illness? Also a brain tumor. She moved away, but we talked on the phone during her final months. I wondered about the "God-extraordinary" connection between the three of us. *Why them and not me?* I do not know why I was spared.

In John 9, Jesus told His disciples that a man had been born blind so "that the works of God should be revealed in him." Then Christ healed the man, an example of the Lord's work in his life. Perhaps my benign tumor was a gift for the intercessors who prayed for me, because their lives were certainly yielded to the Lord. This was one instance where God's saints shared in a rich blessing.

Today, almost twenty years later, the tumor is still there and is still benign. Perhaps the Lord wanted me to be constantly reminded of His glory working in me, reminding me to live a yielded life to the One who spared it.

But You, O Lord, are a shield for me, My glory and the One who lifts up my head. I cried to the Lord with my voice, And He heard me from His holy hill.
I lay down and slept;
I awoke, for the Lord sustained me. (Ps. 3: 3–5)

READER'S NOTES:

_____

_____

_____

_____

_____

_____

In His Time

God sends children for another purpose than merely to keep up the race—to enlarge our hearts; and to make us unselfish and full of kindly sympathies and affections; to give our souls higher aims; to call out all our faculties to extended enterprise and exertion; and to bring round our firesides bright faces, happy smiles, and loving tender hearts. My soul blesses the great Father every day, that he has gladdened the earth with little children.

—Mary Howitt (1799–1888)
English author

In spite of all the infertility treatments available today, many young couples still have heartbreaking difficulty conceiving a child. We have some dear friends who endured that struggle.

Lisa and Jeff had been married about five years. I was in a Bible study with Lisa when she shared their struggle to conceive. She and

Jeff had spent thousands of dollars on some of the most progressive methods available to help couples conceive. Though both of them seemed to be fertile, every method they tried failed. Their struggle was not only a financial strain but also a physical and emotional upheaval.

Lisa loves children. She is a teacher and "Aunt Lisa" to all her friends' children. It was so hard for Lisa to watch her friends' families grow while she faced uncertainty about whether she would ever be a mother herself. Lisa and Jeff had never dismissed the possibility of adoption, but for years they only focused their energies on conceiving a child.

At our Bible study, Lisa fervently poured out the desire of her heart in prayer. She knew the Lord could grant her wish to have a child yet was unsure that He would. As months passed, Lisa's heart changed. Her desire became not her will but God's. She totally yielded to His will for her, no matter what the outcome.

As this change was taking place in Lisa's heart, Jeff and Lisa began to strongly feel that the Lord was leading them to actively pursue adoption. Now they faced the challenge of finding a newborn available for adoption. Finally they found an agency that gave them hope. Jeff and Lisa filled out pages of biographical information, gathered character references, and granted home interviews to case workers. They felt like they were under constant scrutiny.

This particular agency allowed pregnant mothers to read intimate profiles of prospective adoptive parents. Lisa's information about church, tea parties, and ballet captured the attention of one young girl who decided that Jeff and Lisa were the parents she wanted for her unborn child.

In August of that year Jeff and Lisa brought home baby Bonnie.

After seven years of anticipated arrival, this was indeed a happy homecoming!

At Thanksgiving Jeff stood up in church to share the blessing of their adopted baby girl. He said, "If God had allowed us to conceive our own child on our timetable and not His, then we wouldn't have received God's gift of Bonnie, and not having Bonnie would be unacceptable."

Two months later Jeff and Lisa conceived their own child. Their son, Connor, was born in September, a little more than a year after Bonnie arrived home.

What a blessing it has been to see how God worked to create this family in His time and in His way. God's plan certainly exceeded any expectations Jeff and Lisa had for their family and produced a greater good. When I grow impatient, I simply remember how the Lord worked in their lives.

> **Through the Lord's mercies we are not consumed, because His compassions fail not. They are new every morning; great is Your faithfulness. "The Lord is my portion," says my soul, "Therefore I hope in Him!"** *The Lord is good to those who wait for Him, to the soul who seeks Him.* **It is good that one should hope and wait quietly for the salvation of the Lord. (Lam. 3:22–26, emphasis added)**

READER'S NOTES:

_____

_____

_____

_____

Auld Lang Syne

Witnessing for Christ is one of the greatest privileges of
life, second only to knowing Him!

—Dr. Edward Pauley
Footsteps to Follow[2]

My husband, Boo, became a Christian five years after we married, but God started working on his heart much sooner. During the
early years of our marriage, Boo and I worked together selling club
memberships designed to fill members' leisure time with travel,
dining, and entertainment. Each year we held a New Year's Eve party
for club members in a lavish setting. One year we were in the Baker
Hotel in downtown Dallas, Texas. We met in the lobby for pre-party
cocktails.

Boo and his friend Bill were standing in the lobby when a
stranger approached them and presented the Gospel to them. Boo

17

was uncomfortable and tried to divert Bill's attention, but Bill stayed and listened.

Fast-forward two years. Boo and I were in our fifth year of marriage; I was pregnant with our first child. We had a different line of work—corporate gifts—but the same lifestyle.

One evening my brother and sister-in-law invited us to attend a neighborhood Bible study with them. Boo reluctantly agreed to go because he knew I wanted to. He grew even more uncomfortable when the Bible study leader, Ben Martin, closed the evening by praying for a healthy pregnancy for me and my unborn child. When Ben finished praying for me, this godly man was moved to pray for Boo. In that moment my husband became a Christian.

As Ben Martin and Boo became friends, Boo soon learned that Ben was the stranger who had first approached him two years earlier on New Year's Eve. This was more evidence that God works when we yield to His will.

Boo's friend Bill had become a believer shortly after his encounter on that New Year's Eve—the first yield.

Boo's salvation—the second yield.

Bill introduced us to a Christian bookstore owner. That encounter changed our business direction from corporate gifts to Christian gifts—the third yield.

The yielding continues, thanks to Ben Martin, who answered a call to witness to two strangers more than twenty-five years ago.

For "whoever calls on the name of the Lord shall be saved." How then shall they call upon Him in whom they have not believed? And how shall they believe in

Him of whom they have not heard? . . . As it is written: "How beautiful are the feet of those who preach the gospel of peace, who bring glad tidings of good things!" (Rom. 10:13–15)

READER'S NOTES:

_____

_____

_____

_____

_____

_____

IS THERE MORE THAN ONE WAY?

When I was young I was sure of everything; in a few years, having been mistaken a thousand times, I was not half so sure of most things as I was before; at present, I am hardly sure of anything but what God has revealed to me.

—John Wesley (1703–91)
Clergyman and founder of Methodism

BY ZIG ZIGLAR

A few months before her untimely death, I spotted my daughter Suzan in my rearview mirror as I was driving to the office. Suzan worked closely with me on my newspaper column, and she, too, was headed for the office. A minute later she drove past me because she was in the fast-moving center lane while I was in the slow-moving right lane. After a short while, I passed her, waving and smiling as I did so. A few blocks later she passed me again. She was grinning quite broadly as if to say, "You see, Dad, the center lane is best after all." But her triumph was short-lived; in a few more blocks I passed her.

By then we were just a few blocks from the office, and traffic was considerably heavier. Suzan missed her turn and sped past me as I turned to head for the office. Just as I pulled into my parking place, Suzan—who had taken the longer route—was pulling into hers.

The first point is, we really should not be too concerned when somebody gets ahead of us, whether in traffic or in life. In the ever-changing landscape of life, the sun often shines on one person for a spell, then shines on another. The second point is, sometimes the shortest or easiest way is not necessarily the best, or even the fastest, way. We must frequently make detours to arrive at our destination. Had Suzan attempted to turn from the center lane, it might have meant disaster. Because she was flexible and willing to detour, she arrived exactly as she had planned. The third point is, we should be willing and excited to learn from the success of others. If someone is able to arrive ahead of us, we should say, "Super good! How'd you do it?" Think about it.

Excerpted from *Something to Smile About* by Zig Ziglar (Nashville: Thomas Nelson, Inc., 1997), 153–54. Used by permission.

Now Elijah took his mantle, rolled it up, and struck the water; and it was divided this way and that, so that the two of them crossed over on dry ground. And so it was, when they had crossed over, that Elijah said to Elisha, "Ask! What may I do for you, before I am taken away from you?" Elisha said, "Please let a double portion of your spirit be upon me." So he said, "You have asked a hard thing. Nevertheless, if you see me when I am taken from you, it shall be so for you; but if not, it shall not be so." Then it happened, as they continued on and talked, that suddenly a chariot of fire appeared with horses of fire, and separated the two of them; and Elijah went up by a whirlwind into heaven. And Elisha saw it, and cried out, "My father, my father, the chariot of Israel and its horsemen!" So he saw him no more. And he took hold of his own clothes and tore them into two pieces. He also took up the mantle of Elijah that had fallen from him, and went back and stood by the bank of the Jordan. Then he took the mantle of Elijah that had fallen from him, and struck the water, and said, "Where is the Lord God of Elijah?" And when he also had struck the water, it was divided this way and that; and Elisha crossed over. (2 Kings 2:8–14)

READER'S NOTES:

_____

_____

_____

_____

_____

_____

THE SOURCE OF MY STRENGTH

<hr>

Not in the achievement, but in the endurance of the human soul, does it show its divine grandeur, and its alliance with the infinite God.

—E.H. Chapin (1814–80)
American clergyman

BY TERRY MEEUWSEN

*T*he Hiding Place chronicles the life of Corrie ten Boom. Corrie and her family were Dutch believers who hid Jews in their home during the Nazi reign of terror. They were finally arrested and imprisoned for hiding and smuggling Jews to safety. Corrie was the only survivor.

When I consider the condition of the world today—the loss of high moral standards, the increasing instances of violence and drug use, and the basic disregard for human life—I am frightened for our nation and am deeply concerned for my children. In a world where rules are scorned and personal rights take precedence over all else, how do I teach my children that some things are worth dying for? Stories like Corrie's help me to keep on keeping on in my own faith walk and to encourage my children in theirs.

Years ago, at the age of twenty-two, a friend encouraged me to enter the Miss America Pageant. I wanted to study professionally in New York City, and the pageant scholarship was substantial enough to make that dream a reality.

But there was a process to it. You had to enter a local pageant first. If you won that, you competed in Atlantic City, New Jersey, for the Miss America title. Oh, the effort I put into that endeavor! It took hours, days, months of discipline and perseverance. There were mock interviews, rehearsals, and workouts. There were sessions on walking, wardrobe, cosmetics, and speech. And singing, singing, singing.

Ultimately I won, and I was given many opportunities and blessings as a result of being Miss America. But I did all that for a crown that will perish. How much more should I be willing to do for a crown that is imperishable?

The Bible is filled with stories of men and women who, in the face of impossible circumstances, persevered and were mightily used by God. I want to be the kind of woman God can count on. Yet when I look at my own weaknesses or the circumstances around me, I am discouraged. I look at my children and the challenges that face them, and I am afraid. But then I lift my eyes to my heavenly Father and am reminded that He is strong.

In *The Hiding Place,* Corrie expresses her fear to her father and asks how she can be sure she'll have the courage to live out her faith if her family is caught. Her father says, "Corrie, when we take a train ride, when do you get the ticket to get on the train?"

Corrie answered, "When the train is ready to leave."

So it is with our God. We receive the strength to walk the walk when the time comes. We need to keep our heart's attitude right, but the ability and strength to persevere will come from Him.

Excerpted from *Near to the Heart of God* by Terry Meeuwsen (Nashville: Thomas Nelson, Inc., 1998), 74–76. Used by permission.

Now to Him who is able to do exceedingly abundantly above all that we ask or think, according to the power that works in us, to Him be the glory in the church by Christ Jesus to all generations, forever and ever. Amen. (Eph. 3:20–21)

READER'S NOTES:

_____

_____

_____

_____

_____

_____

WHAT HAPPENS
WHEN MOTHERS PRAY?

All the duties of religion are eminently solemn and vener-
able in the eyes of children. But none will so strongly
prove the sincerity of the parent; none so powerfully
awaken the reverence of the child; none so happily rec-
ommend the instruction he receives, as family devotions,
particularly those in which petitions for the children
occupy a distinguished place.

—Timothy Dwight (1752–1817)
American theologian

Have you ever been so devoted to prayer that your "intuition"
served as a signal to pray?

The women's Bible study leaders at my church recently spent
several weeks preparing for a study on prayer. Carol Brewer, our

pastor's wife, shared an experience she felt resulted from the constancy of prayer during that study.

One day she was talking to a friend on the phone when thoughts of her teenage daughter, Becca, overwhelmed her. Becca had gone to school that morning a little anxious about the events facing her that evening. This would be a night of firsts for Becca: her first dance, first semiformal dress, first date, a new hairdo. Carol's feeling that she should pray immediately for Becca were so strong, Carol interrupted her phone conversation and asked her friend to join her in praying for Becca.

When Becca came home that afternoon, Carol asked about her day. Becca said that during one of her classes, she had gotten so nervous about the upcoming school dance, she wanted to cry and felt like she was going to be sick.

Carol asked, "What time was that, Becca?"

Becca answered, "During fourth period, right before lunch—about 11:30, I guess. But I got over it quickly and felt better the rest of the day."

What time did Carol and her friend pray for Becca? You guessed it: 11:30.

Continue earnestly in prayer, being vigilant in it with thanksgiving. (Col. 4:2)

READER'S NOTES:

_____

_____

REKINDLING THE FLAME

God is great, and therefore he will be sought: He is good,
and therefore He will be found.

—John Jay (1745–1829)
Chief Justice, U.S. Supreme Court

BY MICHAEL W. SMITH

W hen I was in high school, most of my closest friends were
several years older than I. Several were fellow church members. By
the time I reached my junior year, they were away at college or off
on their own. Most maintained a strong relationship with the Lord,
but some didn't. They left our small town and got caught up in
things that were contrary to the way we were raised.

At the time, I was on fire for God and pretty idealistic. I just
couldn't believe they could get sidetracked. I thought about all
the great times we'd shared—the church youth musicals, the

trips, the fellowship times, the impromptu prayer meetings at our house. How could they walk away from the things they knew to be true?

Then I moved away from Kenova, West Virginia, and fell into some of the same patterns. While playing in bar bands in Nashville, I lived in a series of pretty crummy places. In those days, my parents made frequent trips to see me. My mom, bless her heart, would bring her sewing machine and sew curtains to try to make whatever dump I was living in seem a little more like home.

Spiritually, I was in some pretty crummy places too. I was a total night owl, playing in a Holiday Inn lounge until two or three in the morning, then sleeping most of the day. The people I hung around with were hardly encouraging. In fact, one of my room-mates sold drugs.

During those dark days, the flame of my faith was barely flickering, and I was doing nothing to fuel it. My family and friends back home understood some of what was going on in my life, but they knew that as an adult I had to make my own decisions. I'm sure their thoughts were similar to my thoughts about my friends only a few years before . . .

Things turned around for me when I hit bottom after a bad experience with drugs and realized just how desperately I needed God. I totally relate to David's words in Psalm 34:17–18:

The righteous cry out, and the Lord hears,
And delivers them out of all their troubles.
The Lord is near to those who have a broken heart,
And saves such as have a contrite spirit.

Within a few months of bottoming out, the Lord opened the door for me to leave the bar band and begin traveling with the Christian group Higher Ground. He started rekindling the fire of faith within me.

Excerpted from *Your Place in This World* by Michael W. Smith (Nashville: Thomas Nelson, Inc., 1998), 143–146. Used by permission.

O Lord, You have searched me and known me.
You know my sitting down and my rising up;
You understand my thought from afar off.
You comprehend my path and my lying down,
And are acquainted with all my ways.
For there is not a word on my tongue,
But behold, O Lord, You know it altogether.
You have hedged me behind and before,
And laid Your hand upon me.
Such knowledge is too wonderful for me;
It is high, I cannot attain it. (Ps. 139:1–6)

READER'S NOTES:

_____
_____
_____
_____
_____
_____

Y2J Yield to Jesus

Conviction Is the Key

"One *can't* believe impossible things."

"I daresay you haven't had much practice," said the Queen. "When I was your age, I always did it for half an hour a day. Why, sometimes I've believed as many as six impossible things before breakfast."[3]

—Lewis Carroll [Charles Lutwidge Dodgson] (1832–1898)
British writer, mathematician

BY ZIG ZIGLAR

The late Mary Crowley frequently commented that one person with a conviction could do more than a hundred who only had an interest. Commitment is the key to staying the course and completing the project. Conviction always precedes commitment.

When you're convinced as a salesperson that you are selling a marvelous product, your demeanor, body language, voice inflection, and facial expressions communicate to the prospective customer that

31

you fervently believe you're offering something of value. Many times the customer will buy, not because of her belief in the product, goods, or service, but because of the salesperson's belief in the product.

Our feelings are transferable. Courage can be, and frequently is, transferred to the other person. Convictions are the same. The teacher who fervently believes in the message he delivers will persuade the student by the very depth of that conviction. One of my favorite Mary Kay Ash quotes is, "Many people have gone a lot farther than they thought they could because someone else thought they could." In short, their confidence, born of someone else's conviction, enabled them to make it. Conviction comes from knowledge and a feeling that what we're teaching, doing or selling is absolutely right. When we transfer that conviction to others within our sphere of influence, they benefit, as does society.

Show me a person with deep convictions, and I'll show you a person who has made a commitment to deliver those convictions to others. Show me a great leader, and I'll show you a person with deep convictions who is able to attract followers because of those convictions. I'll also show you a person who is happy in what she is doing and far more successful than people who do not have those convictions. Message: Buy that idea, develop those convictions, and make that commitment.

Excerpted from *Something to Smile About* by Zig Ziglar (Nashville: Thomas Nelson, Inc., 1997), 41–42. Used by permission.

**Not that I have already attained, or am already perfected;
but I press on, that I may lay hold of that for which Christ**

Jesus has also laid hold of me. Brethren, I do not count myself to have apprehended; but one thing I do, forgetting those things which are behind and reaching forward to those things which are ahead, I press toward the goal for the prize of the upward call of God in Christ Jesus. Therefore let us, as many as are mature, have this mind; and if in anything you think otherwise, God will reveal even this to you. Nevertheless, to the degree that we have already attained, let us walk by the same rule, let us be of the same mind. (Phil. 3:12–16)

READER'S NOTES:

_____

_____

_____

_____

_____

_____

A TIME TO DIE

Death marks the beginning, not the end. It is our journey
to God.

—Billy Graham (1918–)
American evangelist

ennie lived a fruitful life as a strong Christian. When she was
ninety-eight, a series of ministrokes forced her family to place her in
a nursing home. As her earthly body shut down, Dennie lapsed into
a coma that lasted several days. Her family surrounded her constantly. Even though Dennie had lived a full life, they weren't ready
to let her go, and perhaps she didn't want to let go either. She held
on, day after day.

One day Dennie's granddaughter-in-law, Dea, was driving home
from work when she had an overwhelming urge to visit Dennie. Dea
began comforting Dennie by gently caressing her arm and singing a

favorite hymn: "And He walks with me, and He talks with me, and He tells me I am His own . . ."⁴ When Dea finished singing, Dennie opened her eyes but still didn't speak. Dea felt the Lord's presence and an incredible peace surrounding them.

Dea looked into Dennie's dear face, recalling the many changes Dennie had seen during ninety-eight years—from getting married in a horse and buggy to watching men walk in space. Dennie had raised her family and watched it grow to four generations.

Dea spoke softly to Dennie from her heart, sharing thoughts about her own family. She knew Dennie loved her grandchildren deeply, and she told her how wonderful it was that Dennie had been alive to know and hold Dea's last child. Dea said she knew Dennie was worried about leaving her family behind, but she asked Dennie not to worry—all the children would be loved and cared for, and the family would keep Dennie's memory alive. Dea assured Dennie it was all right to let go. The next day Dennie Henson went home to be with her Lord.

Many of us have known people who seem to hang on until they find peace about leaving loved ones or until they have taken care of some last-minute details to ease the pain for those left behind. My husband, Boo, lost his father three weeks after we were married. We lived in New Orleans, 500 miles away from Boo's family. Boo's mother called to tell us the end was near and asked Boo to come as quickly as possible. It was evening, and there were no flights to Dallas from New Orleans, so Boo drove all night to reach his father's bedside. When Boo walked into his father's hospital room, his father opened his eyes in recognition, murmuring Boo's nickname that was an endearment to them both. Moments later, he died.

It is a precious gift when God allows us to linger until we can "tie up loose ends" or have a final moment with a precious loved one. But we shouldn't leave behind loose ends or regrets, in case death is sudden. Keep short accounts with friends and family. Don't leave behind words of anger or unwritten letters. Plan to leave behind words of blessing and good memories: a yielded life.

Death will be a beginning for all of us who believe. The only things we can take with us are our relationships with family and friends. Let our words and daily lives make them want to join us in eternity. Are *you* ready for your journey home to God?

> **For to me to live is Christ, and to die is gain. But if I live on in the flesh, this will mean fruit from my labor; yet what I shall choose I cannot tell. For I am hard-pressed between the two, having a desire to depart and be with Christ, which is far better. Nevertheless to remain in the flesh is more needful for you. And being confident of this, I know that I shall remain and continue with you all for your progress and joy of faith, that your rejoicing for me may be more abundant in Jesus Christ by my coming to you again. (Phil. 1:21–26)**

READER'S NOTES:

_____

_____

_____

_____

MUCH AFRAID NO MORE

It is only the fear of God that can deliver us from the fear
of man.

—John Witherspoon (1723–94)
Scottish-American clergyman

Can you imagine growing up afraid of everything that moves or makes noise? In the imagination of a child afraid of sound or movement, a television, a vacuum cleaner, a car, or water washing down a bathtub drain can be monstrous. This is how Jeanne Kumbier lived her childhood.

Because of her fears and unusual behavior, Jeanne's parents were afraid she was autistic until she began to speak. Even then they knew something was different about Jeanne. One psychologist suggested she had childhood schizophrenia. A psychiatrist said Jeanne was neither schizophrenic nor autistic, but had an anxiety disorder.

He told Jeanne's parents to treat her normally and not pressure her about her fears. Jeanne's parents were relieved but still wondered if their daughter would ever live a normal life.

In spite of her fears and adjustment problems, Jeanne became aware of God's love and protection at an early age. She asked Jesus to come into her heart when she was five. Even at that age she knew God was real and that she needed Him. She learned to pray about her fears and eventually overcame many of them.

In her teens, Jeanne became confused about God's love. When things got rough at school, she thought God had abandoned her or that somehow she deserved all the trouble. To Jeanne, it seemed that God was always angry with His people. When people made fun of her, she wondered if God also was laughing at her.

Toward the end of high school, Jeanne became depressed and more fearful. At home she was withdrawn and explosive—even self-destructive, actually striking herself and beating her head against the wall. She lay awake many nights wondering where God was. She truly wanted to die.

Yet, she didn't totally give up; instead, she told her parents she needed help. They found a psychiatrist who was able to help Jeanne change her behavior and thought patterns. She progressed so well that she was able to attend college that fall.

Life seemed to improve for Jeanne at college. She made friends and excelled academically, but she still felt spiritually barren. She still doubted whether God was actually a loving God.

Some of Jeanne's new friends were strong Christians; they felt led to pray for her and explain the Gospel to her. In 1989, the night before Easter, Jeanne received the assurance of her salvation. She realized that God loved her more than she could understand and that she needed to let Him control her life. She surrendered her life to Him, realizing He had been with her all along, protecting her and leading her back to Himself.

Recently Jeanne learned her childhood problem has a name: hyperlexia—a little-known syndrome similar to autism. This revelation has helped bring closure to the trauma of that dark period in her life.

At twenty-seven, Jeanne occasionally has bad days, but now there are more good days than bad. Whenever she gets discouraged, when things don't change quickly enough as she deals with the fears in her life, she remembers the times in her life when she couldn't go anywhere alone, get a job, communicate, make friends, drive on a freeway, or cope with a normal day. Jeanne believes God alone enabled her to do normal things. With Christ in her life, she is able to live on her own, go to school, drive a car, or just tie her shoes—things that once seemed impossible. Yielding and trusting in God's power makes accomplishing what we consider ordinary tasks extraordinary to Jeanne.

I will mention the lovingkindnesses of the Lord and the praises of the Lord, according to all that the Lord has bestowed on us, and the great goodness toward the house of Israel, which He has bestowed on them according to His mercies, according to the multitude of His lovingkindnesses . . . In all their affliction He was afflicted, and the Angel of His Presence saved them; in His love and in His pity He redeemed them;

and He bore them and carried them all the days of old.
(Isa. 63:7, 9)

READER'S NOTES:

_____

_____

_____

_____

_____

_____

WHO CAN BE AGAINST US?

Christianity works while infidelity talks. She feeds the hungry, clothes the naked, visits and cheers the sick, and seeks the lost, while infidelity abuses her and babbles nonsense and profanity. "By their fruits ye shall know them."
—Henry Ward Beecher (1813–37)
American clergyman

Mark Engelthaler, a pastor in my church, went to the Ukraine on a teaching trip. One of his students, Valia, shared her testimony.

Valia is from Rumania. She and her siblings were orphaned when Valia was ten. As the oldest sister, she became responsible for caring for the household. Her older brother left their rural area to find work in the city so he could support the family.

One day her brother went into a shoe-repair shop, and the Christians who owned the shop led him to the Lord. He wrote Valia and told her about his changed life. One evening shortly afterward, Valia prayed on her own to accept Christ.

Unable to contain her newfound joy, Valia told everyone in her community about her new life. Her small hometown was primarily Russian Orthodox. Two local priests warned Valia to talk about her faith and God only through them. But Valia had found a Bible and continued to talk about the Lord and read her Bible aloud to her friends and neighbors. It didn't seem to bother anyone except the priests—they were infuriated. They ordered her to stop her "preaching" immediately. Valia refused.

The priests decided to make an example of Valia's rebellion. They tied her to a pole in the middle of town, intending to *burn her at the stake!* However, when they tried to douse her with gasoline siphoned from a gas tank, the hose line clogged. They attempted several times to unclog the line to no avail. Finally, the embarrassed priests untied her and chased her away. Later that month, the two priests died, presumably of natural causes.

Valia yielded to her Lord. Who can come against that?

If God is for us, who can be against us? He who did not spare His own Son, but delivered Him up for us all, how shall He not with Him also freely give us all things? Who shall bring a charge against God's elect? It is God who justifies. Who is he who condemns? It is Christ who died, and furthermore is also risen, who is even at the right hand of God, who makes intercession for us. Who shall separate us from the love of Christ? Shall tribulation, or distress, or persecution, or famine, or

nakedness, or peril, or sword? . . . Yet in all these things we are more than conquerors through Him who loved us. (Rom. 8:31b–35, 37)

_____
_____
_____
_____
_____
_____

CREATING WONDER

He that does good to another, does also good to himself;
not only in the consequence, but in the very act of doing
it; for the consciousness of welldoing is an ample reward.
—Seneca (4 B.C.–A.D. 65)
Roman Stoic philosopher

I enjoy hearing about random acts of kindness, and I often think about the effect these acts have on their recipients. The "random" act is usually quite intentional on the part of the giver, who yields to an inner nudge.

My husband, Boo, and I own a company that manufactures Christian gift products. Most of our items are framed pictures that incorporate encouraging Scriptures. One Sunday near Christmas, Boo, our son, Cord, and I were returning home from church; some of our products just "happened" to be in the car. I mentioned one picture

44

that was a favorite and remarked that it might even appeal to non-churchgoers. This triggered the "nudge" compartment of Boo's brain.

He steered the car from the main street into a quiet neighborhood. It was a beautiful day, and many people had their front doors open so they could see outside.

Boo did not reveal his intentions immediately. We drove around for a while, and then he shared his plan: He would pull up in front of a home, and Cord would take a picture to the homeowner as a gift from an anonymous benefactor.

Amazingly, Cord had absolutely no reservations about his role in this adventure. He walked to a front door, knocked, and waited. The woman who came to the door must have wondered what he was selling. When Cord extended the decorative picture and explained that "someone" wanted her to have it, a range of emotions crossed her face. She was puzzled but still admired the picture, delighted that it was for her. She accepted it and thanked our son for bringing it by.

When was the last time you responded at random to the Lord's leading? The next time you are nudged, yield.

He who sows sparingly will also reap sparingly, and he who sows bountifully will also reap bountifully. *So let each one give as he purposes in his heart,* **not grudgingly or of necessity; for God loves a cheerful giver. (2 Cor. 9:6–7, emphasis added)**

READER'S NOTES:

_____

_____

OUT OF AFRICA

I have benefited by praying for others; for by making an
errand to God for them I have gotten something for myself.
—Samuel Rutherford (1600–61)
Scottish clergyman

*A missionary from Michigan shared this story (while home on furlough)
to illustrate the value of prayer.*

"While I was serving at a small field hospital in Africa, every
two weeks I rode my bicycle through the jungle to a nearby city for
supplies. This is a two-day journey, and I had to camp overnight. On
one of these trips, I planned to withdraw money from the bank to
purchase medicine and supplies.

"Upon my arrival, I saw two men fighting. One of them was
seriously injured. I treated his injuries and witnessed to him about
the Lord Jesus Christ. Then I went back home.

"Two weeks later I repeated my journey. When I got to the city, the young man I had treated approached me. He told me that he knew I carried money and medicines. He said, 'Some friends and I followed you into the jungle, knowing you would camp overnight. We planned to kill you and take your money and drugs. But just as we were about to move into your camp, we saw that you were surrounded by twenty-six armed guards.'

"At this I laughed and said that I was certainly all alone in that jungle campsite. The young man insisted, 'No sir, I wasn't the only person to see the guards. My five friends also saw them, and we all counted them. It was because of those guards that we were afraid and left you alone.'"

At this point in the missionary's story, a man in the congregation jumped to his feet and interrupted the missionary. The man asked, "Can you tell me the date this happened?" The missionary told the date, and the man told him this story:

"On the night of your incident in Africa, it was morning here, and I was playing golf. I was about to putt when I felt the urge to pray for you. In fact, the urge was so strong, I called men in this church to meet me here in the sanctuary to pray for you. Would everyone who met me that day stand up?"

The men who had met to pray stood up. The missionary counted them. *There were 26.*

Put on the whole armor of God, that you may be able to stand against the wiles of the devil. For we do not wrestle against flesh and blood, but against principalities, against powers, against the rulers of the darkness

of this age . . . praying always with all prayer and supplication in the Spirit, being watchful to this end with all perseverance and supplication for all the saints. (Eph. 6:11–12, 18)

2-26-05

READER'S NOTES:

Don't forget the importance of
intercessory prayer

THE GUIDEBOOK

Holy Bible, Book divine,
Precious treasure, thou art mine:
Mine to tell me whence I came;
Mine to teach me what I am.

—John Burton Sr. (1773–1822)

BY CYNTHIA HEALD

The Bible is *the* guidebook to the heart of God. It tells us everything we need to know about how to make this journey. It gives direction; it teaches; it corrects; it trains. It is God's Holy Spirit-breathed book for us to read, study, and meditate on. Through consistent intake of Scripture, we will grow strong. Here we will find the revelation of our heavenly Father's character. Here we will discover His love for His people.

Every parent has heard the familiar excuse, "Oh, Mom, I didn't know you wanted me to do that!" We can never say to God, "I didn't know! If only You had told me!" All of His instructions to us are in His Word, carefully preserved for our encouragement and use . . . I would like to share with you some insights that others have taught me, and that I have discovered firsthand to be very fruitful, about how to use the Bible to guide us in our journey to the heart of the Father.

A reader's delight. To spend time daily in the Scriptures, I have always used a yearly Bible reading plan. (Some people find it helpful to use a one-year Bible.) I need a schedule that tells me what to read on a specific day—and besides, if I didn't have a plan, I would never be likely to read Leviticus! I have found it important to be flexible. If I miss a day or two, I don't try to catch up; I go ahead and read the current day's selection. I may not read everything in a one-year plan, but I know that over a year's time, my reading will be much more consistent as a result.

There is a place for studying the Bible, but I especially love just *reading* it. I'm not analyzing specific words, cross-referencing texts, or studying theology; I'm just reading. It's the Bible, me, and the Holy Spirit. I smiled when I heard someone comment, "The Bible is the only book in the world that when you read it, the Author shows up!" Jesus declared that the Spirit would be our Guide to the Guidebook: "But when the Father sends the Counselor as my representative—and by the Counselor I mean the Holy Spirit—he will teach you everything and will remind you of everything I myself have told you" (John 14:26 NLT).

Does this mean I understand everything I read? Absolutely not. Having a study Bible or a commentary can be very helpful in explaining difficult passages. But when I read, I essentially open my Bible and pray very simply, "Open my eyes to see the wonderful truths in your law" (Ps. 119:18 NLT). I keep a journal in which I write down what I think God is saying to me in the Scriptures. I always try to learn something from what I read—an instruction I need to apply to my life, a comment concerning God's character and ways, or perhaps an example of how someone responded to Him . . .

What can you do to increase your enjoyment of reading God's Word? The Bible's "living power" guarantees that it will always have fresh truth for my life. Someone has said, "The Word of God will stand a thousand readings, and he who has gone over it most frequently is the surest of finding new wonders there." Years ago I was reading Ruth, which at the time had already become one of my favorite books. As I read Ruth 3:11, I was struck by Boaz's declaration to her: "All my people in the city know that you are a woman of excellence" (NASB). I remember putting my Bible down and saying, "Lord, when did You put that verse in there? I never saw it before!"

A word for my life. Every January, I ask the Lord what He wants to do in my life in the new year. What does He want to teach me? What needs to be changed? As I pray, either a need becomes very obvious or a verse is brought to my attention. When I realize my need—for example, my prayer life or my speech—I find an appropriate verse. I write the verse on a piece of paper the size of a bookmark, which I place my Bible. I memorize the verse, and every day for a year I use the bookmark to prompt me to pray for that verse to become part of my life for the rest of my journey.

This practice has had an incredible impact on my life. God's Word is alive and active, and it penetrates and discloses my thoughts and motives. This year I am praying Proverbs 31:26 in *The Message* rendition: "When she speaks she has something worthwhile to say, and she always says it kindly." Certainly, this is a lifelong project, but my hope is that during this twelve-month period my speech might become a little more considerate, discreet, and discerning . . .

I am convinced that the more time we spend in God's Word, the more we will understand Job's fervent declaration, "I have treasured the words of His mouth more than my necessary food" (Job 23:12 NASB). I read the Word of God, I study it, I memorize it, and I meditate on it because I love it, and because I want to grow and learn and be changed into His image. I do not consider this a spiritual discipline in the sense that it is something that *should* and *ought to* be done. I spend time with the Lord and His Word because doing so is the joy and delight of my heart. His Word is ever new, and His Spirit continually teaches and transforms me. Why would anything this world offers or demands keep me from the eternal richness and blessing of being with, and listening to, my Lord? This Guidebook is the ultimate guidebook, and it leads me straight to the heart of God.

Excerpted from *A Woman's Journey to the Heart of God* by Cynthia Heald (Nashville: Thomas Nelson, Inc., 1997), 59–61, 65–66. Used by permission.

Your word is a lamp to my feet and a light to my path.
(Ps. 119:105)

READER'S NOTES:

_____

_____

_____

_____

Y2J Yield to Jesus

MOTIVATION OF THE HEART

████████████████████████████████████

> One truly Christian life will do more to prove the divine
> origin of Christianity than many lectures. It is of much
> greater importance to develop the Christian character,
> than to exhibit Christian evidences.
>
> —J.M. Gibson (b. 1838)
> Scottish-English-Canadian-American clergyman

During my high school days in the early 1960s, *cancer* was a mis-
understood word. I remember so few people actually using the
word in association with anyone's illness that when my band director's wife got "the cancer," most of my friends and I thought she
would "get over it."

While she was in the hospital, I remember filing past her bed
with my fellow band members, assuring each other she would be
well soon. Our band would be entering the state marching contest

the following week, and this night we would perform for our director's wife four floors below her hospital bed on the street below.

She would not be able to attend the contest, but as she wanted to unite us and uplift us in spirit, she handed each of us a shiny new dime to wear in our shoes to remind us that *she* would be praying for our victory at the contest. When we performed for her that evening, each of us had her dime in our shoe.

Days later after many more practices, always with our dimes, we took the long bus ride to our state contest. We not only won that, but the governor also asked us to travel to New Orleans that year to represent Texas in the Mardi Gras Parade.

That February was bittersweet. We marched the six-mile parade route down Canal Street in New Orleans, there because of the fervent, unselfish prayer of a godly woman. Her victory that year came when she met her Savior, face to face.

"And the things of earth will grow strangely dim in the light of His glory and grace."[5]

We give thanks to God always for you all, making mention of you in our prayers, remembering without ceasing your work of faith, labor of love, and patience of hope in our Lord Jesus Christ in the sight of our God and Father, knowing, beloved brethren, your election by God. (1 Thess. 1:2–4)

READER'S NOTES:

_____

_____

ANTIFREEZE SMOOTHIE

A child of God should be a visible beatitude for joy and hap-
piness, and a living doxology for gratitude and adoration.
—Charles Haddon Spurgeon (1834–92)
English clergyman

Many years ago before cellular phones, pagers, and answering machines were accessories in our lives, the events of the following story might have not turned out so extraordinarily.

My husband and brother-in-law, Joe, had gone to the airport to pick up a relative. Joe's wife, Toni, was at home with her two- and five-year-old sons. Boys at any age are active and inquisitive, so you can imagine the delight they took in exploring their garage. Five-year-old Kit found a container of antifreeze. Do you remember the commercial with the quip, "Why don't we let Mikey try it?" Something like that must have crossed Kit's mind when he poured a cup of antifreeze for his little brother, Tracy, to drink.

I do not know how antifreeze looked and tasted to my nephew, but whenever I use antifreeze I notice a sweet smell, a syrupy consistency, and the color of a blue-raspberry sno-cone!

My toddling nephew drank the whole thing. His older brother, sensing this might not really be okay, sounded the alarm to his mother. Of course, she called their pediatrician immediately. His office said, "Meet the doctor at Children's Hospital now!" Antifreeze may keep a car's engine from shutting down, but for my nephew, it created a list of deadly threats to his little body.

Toni, now at the hospital, called to tell me the next few hours were most critical, but we had no means to contact Joe and let him know about the situation. I had stayed behind in my home with my own toddler. Helplessly standing in the middle of my kitchen, I looked toward the wall phone and said out loud, *"Lord, have Joe call me!"*

My husband recalls sitting in the restaurant when Joe "suddenly" stood, saying he was going to call Toni. It seemed like only seconds after my quick SOS to God that the phone rang. I grabbed the receiver off the wall, and after my quick hello, I heard Joe ask, "Beverly?"

I excitedly yelled, "Yes!"

Joe said, "I'm sorry, I dialed the wrong number. I was calling Toni to tell her we stopped for lunch."

I quickly told Joe about Tracy, and he was able to make it to the hospital for those first critical hours. Four days later our little Tracy was released from the hospital; he recovered completely.

I admit I was amazed that my brother-in-law "accidentally" called me. When I hung up from that call, I rubbed the gooseflesh on my arms and talked out loud to my wall phone. I mumbled something like, "Wow! I can't believe what just happened."

We often have that reaction to the Lord's divine intervention. Thinking back to that day so many years ago, a tragic thought occurred to me. *What about the times I've missed seeing the Lord's intervention in so many situations?* I confess that in the early days of my desire to live for the Lord, I looked for Him in every area of my life. I was zealous to see Him working. I see those early days as a time when the Lord was "courting" me, and I couldn't wait to see what He would do next. I am saddened to think that I have taken the Lord for granted at times and missed other instances where He orchestrated the details beyond my expectations—and I gave credit elsewhere, not to the Lord.

These days I am passionate with expectation that the Lord will handle the details. When the incredible, or even the not so incredible, happens, the gooseflesh reappears, and I am again saying, "Wow! Can you believe it?" I can't wait to see what He will do next!

> **Be merciful to me, O God, be merciful to me! For my soul trusts in You; and in the shadow of Your wings I will make my refuge, until these calamities have passed by. I will cry to God Most High, to God who performs all things for me. He shall send from heaven and save me; He reproaches the one who would swallow me up. God shall send forth His mercy and His truth. (Ps. 57:1–3)**

READER'S NOTES:

_____

_____

_____

THE LAW OF PROCESS:
LEADERSHIP DEVELOPS DAILY, NOT IN A DAY

> If the Golden Rule is to be preached at all in these modern
> days, when so much of life is devoted to business, it must
> be preached especially in its application to the conduct of
> business.
>
> —Ferdinand S. Schenck (1845–1925)
> American theologian

BY JOHN C. MAXWELL

Anne Scheiber was 101 years old when she died in January of
1995. For years she lived in a tiny, run-down, rent-controlled stu-
dio apartment in Manhattan. The paint on the walls was peeling, and
the old bookcases lining those walls were covered in dust. Rent was
four hundred dollars a month.

Scheiber lived on Social Security and a small monthly pension,
which she started receiving in 1943 when she retired from her job

as an auditor for the Internal Revenue Service. She didn't do very well at the IRS. More specifically, the agency didn't do right by her. Despite having a law degree and doing excellent work, Scheiber was never promoted. And when she retired at age fifty-one, she was making only $3,150 a year.

"She was treated very, very shabbily," said Benjamin Clark, who knew her as well as anyone did. "She really had to fend for herself in every way. It was really quite a struggle."

Scheiber was the model of thrift. She didn't spend money on herself. She didn't buy new furniture when the old pieces she owned wore out. She didn't even subscribe to a newspaper. About once a week, she went to the public library to read the *Wall Street Journal*.

So imagine the surprise of Norman Lamm, the president of Yeshiva University in New York City, when he found out that Anne Scheiber, a little old lady whom he never heard of—and who never attended Yeshiva—left nearly her entire estate to the university.

"When I saw the will, it was mind blowing, such an unexpected windfall," said Lamm. "This woman has become a legend overnight." Anne Scheiber's estate was worth $22 million!

How in the world did a retired spinster build an eight-figure fortune? Here's the answer. By the time she retired from the IRS in 1943, Scheiber had managed to save $5,000. She invested that money in stocks. By 1950, she made enough profit to purchase 1,000 shares of Shering-Plough Corporation stock, then valued at $10,000, and she held on to that stock, letting its value build. Today, those original shares have split enough times to produce 128,000 shares, worth $7.5 million.

Scheiber was successful because she spent most of her life

building her worth. Whether her stocks' values went up or down, she never sold them with the thought, *I'm finished building; now it's time to cash out.* She was in for the long haul, the *really* long haul. When she earned dividends—which grew larger and larger—she reinvested them. She spent her whole lifetime building. While other people worry about running out of funds before the end of their lives, the longer Scheiber lived, the wealthier she became. When it came to finances, Scheiber understood and applied the Law of Process.

Excerpted from *The 21 Irrefutable Laws of Leadership* by John C. Maxwell (Nashville: Thomas Nelson, Inc., 1998), 21–22. Used by permission.

> **Blessed is the man**
> **Who walks not in the counsel of the ungodly,**
> **Nor stands in the path of sinners,**
> **Nor sits in the seat of the scornful;**
> **But his delight is in the law of the Lord,**
> **And in His law he meditates day and night.**
> **He shall be like a tree**
> **Planted by the rivers of water,**
> **That brings forth its fruit in its season,**
> **Whose leaf also shall not wither;**
> **And whatever he does shall prosper. (Ps. 1:1–3)**

READER'S NOTES:

_____

_____

_____

BEYOND THE LIMITS

The very society of joy redoubles it; so that while it lights
upon my friend it abounds upon myself, and the brighter
the candle burns, the more easily will it light mine.

—Robert South (1634–1716)
English clergyman

BY FRANKLIN GRAHAM

God can use a chicken. I was traveling through the airport in
Munich, Germany, with Ricky Skaggs, the renowned bluegrass/
country music artist. Exhausted, we were returning from a trip on
behalf of Operation Christmas Child. We left Sarajevo the day
before at 4:00 A.M. and drove through the rugged Bosnian mountains, down the Dalmatian coast of Croatia to the city of Split,
where we boarded a Croatian Airlines flight to Zagreb for the night.
We slept a few hours, and the next morning caught a 6:00 A.M.
flight to Munich.

It was a cold December day, and we were glad to be inside the airport terminal. We hoped to take advantage of the forty-five-minute layover between flights to do some last-minute Christmas shopping at the airport.

As we hurried through the crowded corridors, we spotted a young woman sitting in a corner, crying. *She probably just said good-bye to her husband,* I thought, and kept walking. You see tears shed at airports all the time. If you stopped every time you saw someone crying, you'd never leave.

I turned to say something to Ricky, but he was gone. I stopped in my tracks, wondering *Where in the world is he?* When I looked around, Ricky was kneeling beside the despondent lady. My shoulders dropped, and, taking a tolerant breath, I walked over to see what was going on.

"Can I help you?" Ricky gently asked her.

I was impatient. *Come on, Ricky,* I said to myself. *We'll never get out of here if you talk to everyone who is crying!*

Ricky patiently questioned the woman, who fortunately spoke English. He learned that she was in transit from another country and had lost her airline ticket. She felt stranded and didn't know what to do.

"Let me see if I can help you," Ricky said. "Come with me."

I'm shy when it comes to approaching a total stranger, but it didn't bother Ricky at all. He took control of the situation and led the woman to an airline official and asked for help. He didn't leave her side until he had complete assurance she would be cared for. As he excused himself, he wished her a merry Christmas, then headed back my way with a grin all over his face.

He walked up alongside, slapped me on the back, and said, "You know, Franklin, 'Christmastime's a comin'" (the title of a bluegrass song he sings).

I shook my head, knowing in my heart that the little interruption really hadn't inconvenienced us at all. We still had plenty of time to do our shopping and board the plane on time. Later, as we rumbled down the runway for takeoff, I felt convicted. Even after spending several days reaching out to the hurting, the poor, and the anguished, I let my heart grow a little bit hard.

But Ricky showed me that the compassion he is known for is always in season and knows no limit. In other words, he walks the talk. Just as God never closes His eyes, we should keep our eyes open so that God can help us go beyond the limits of our human frailties.

Satan is always trying to rob us of these moments of availability. He'll rob us by saying: "You're tired, you need your rest." "You're busy." "Of course you'd like to help, but you just don't have time." "Take a look at your watch. If you get involved, you'll miss your next appointment."

But on the way home, I remembered a story that Sami Dagher shared with me, a story that speaks powerfully of how we can step beyond the limits and be used mightily by Him when we reach out to others.

The big fish. In the late seventies, Sami Dagher woke up in the middle of the night from a restless sleep, troubled by his spirit. Lebanon was in the midst of a vicious civil war between the Muslim PLO and the Lebanese Christians. "Lord," he prayed, "give me an opportunity to share my faith with somebody today."

Later that morning, Sami got in his Volkswagen microbus, heading to his office. As he drove through the narrow and crowded streets of Beirut, he noticed a strange sight—a Syrian army officer hitchhiking. Sami couldn't remember seeing a Syrian officer hitchhiking in Lebanon before, and for good reason—he was as likely to catch a bullet as he was a ride. At this stage in the Lebanese civil war, Syria was siding with the PLO, funneling guns and ammunition to the guerrillas. They later switched allegiances and came in later as reputed peacekeepers; in reality, they simply hoped to get a piece of Sami's beloved Lebanon.

Sami saw the soldier and immediately became indignant. *No way would I ever give him a ride,* Sami thought. *Why don't those Syrians leave us alone? They've caused enough trouble.*

As Sami drove past the soldier, something inside made him slow down. He remembered his restless sleep and his prayer in the middle of the night: "Lord, give me an opportunity to share my faith with somebody today."

Ah, a big fish, Sami thought, as he looked into the rearview mirror. *God is giving me a big fish.* Sami turned his van around and pulled onto the gravel embankment, stopping just in front of the Syrian officer. Understandably, the soldier was wary at first, but he saw Sami's warm expression and climbed into the van.

"Where are you headed?" Sami asked.

The officer told him, and though he was headed in a slightly different direction from where Sami planned to go, Sami said, "I'll take you there."

Sami had his big fish on the hook. He didn't waste any time engaging the officer in conversation, and quickly got to the subject weighing most heavily on his heart. As Sami neared the destination, he noticed that it was getting close to the noon hour. Sami didn't feel that he said all he needed to say—he needed more time to present the gospel. "Have you had lunch?" he asked the officer.

"No."

"You would honor my home with your presence if you would have lunch with me," Sami said. The Syrian officer's forehead wrinkled up like a well-worn map. It was surprising enough that a Lebanese Christian would give him a ride. But lunch?

Sami encouraged him. The Syrian smiled in spite of himself. "OK, I'll come," he said.

Sami's heart leaped. But he quickly realized there was no time to notify his wife, Joy. He stopped at the roadside grill along the way and bought a roasted chicken.

At home, Sami's wife cheerfully prepared a typical Lebanese meal—charcoal chicken and flat pita bread with some fresh raw vegetables. Sami kept serving generous portions of chicken to the Syrian officer; the longer the man ate, the longer Sami had to tell him about what Christ had done for him. Sami fed his guest every morsel of chicken to keep him occupied, wondering all the while if anything he was saying was sinking in. When the chicken was gone, the man pushed back from the table and said, "Thank you, I must be on my way."

The officer had shown no emotion as Sami shared the gospel. He didn't seem angry, but neither did he seem particularly interested. He just listened politely. Sami got up, dismayed, but drove the man to where he needed to go and waved good-bye.

Sami never saw him again. He felt that perhaps he failed; maybe he should have bought two chickens! Or maybe he just took the wrong approach. Regardless of the lack of response, Sami was thankful that God gave him an opportunity to share his faith just as he asked in his prayer.

The rest of the story. Sami wanted the Syrian officer to get on his knees immediately and ask Christ to come into his life, but God had other plans. Sami was left to wonder about his witness. Paul Harvey is famous for hanging his audience in suspense as he tells his behind-the-scene stories. He keeps you guessing until the fabulous wrap, "And now, the rest of the story."

The rest of the story for Sami Dagher and the Syrian soldier is remarkable. To live beyond our limits is to be on God's timetable. Often that means we must be patient.

Several years after Sami offered a ride and a chicken lunch to the Syrian officer, a young Christian dentist living in Damascus decided to open his own clinic. Before he was allowed to do that, however, the Syrian socialist government required him to complete several years of government service. The young dentist was assigned to a little mud village in the eastern district, near the Iraqi border. He began using every opportunity to tell his patients about the love of Jesus Christ. After all, he reasoned, in the dentist's chair they were certainly a captive audience, and they couldn't very well argue back when he had his hands and instruments in their mouths.

There are safer places in the world to share your faith in Christ than in Syria. Word soon spread among the villagers about the Christian dentist in their midst. When it became clear that the young man would neither renounce his faith nor stop talking about it, the local religious leaders decided to punish him.

There was just one problem. Since the dentist worked for the government, he was technically a government employee. Harming a government employee, however, has its own consequences, so the religious leaders approached the military police, urging them to bring charges against this man so they could legitimize their persecution.

The officer in charge was obligated to interrogate the dentist. For you to understand what happened next, you must completely erase any notion of *interrogation* that you may have from watching police shows on television. In Syria, interrogation can be worse than death.

The young dentist was prepared for interrogation by being "softened up," which meant they whipped him, beat him, kicked him, and then began asking questions.

"Who are you?" the soldiers demanded, and the dentist gave them his name.

"Where are you from?"

"Damascus."

"What are you?"

"I'm a Christian. I belong to the Church of Damascus."

The Syrian officer leading the interrogation immediately shouted, "Stop!" and ordered every military man out of the room. The dentist swallowed hard.

This man's going to kill me, he thought, *and there won't be any witnesses.*

When the room was cleared, the officer leaned over his chair and asked, "Do you know a man in Beirut by the name of Sami Dagher?"

The young dentist did know Sami, because Sami had preached in his church. But how in the world could this officer know Sami? *Oh, no,* the dentist gulped. *What has Sami done now? And what will happen to me since I know him?*

As a believer, the dentist knew he couldn't lie, so with a hushed reluctance he looked at his interrogator. "Yes, I know Sami Dagher."

"If you know Sami Dagher of Beirut," the officer stood tall, "you're free to go and continue your work."

The dentist let out a sigh of shocked relief as the officer told him how, several years earlier, Sami Dagher picked him up and gave him a chicken for lunch. During that lunch, the officer recounted, Sami told him the "most wonderful" story that he had ever heard in his life; the story of a Savior who came out of heaven to this earth to die for the sins of this world. If the officer would believe in this Savior, his own wrongdoings could be forgiven.

"I've had a sweet taste in my mouth ever since," he told the young dentist. "I have never forgotten his words."

The Syrian officer never gave the dentist any indication that he had become a Christian, but because of Sami's faithfulness and obedience, even to an enemy, the officer spared the young dentist. Two years earlier, when Sami prayed for the opportunity to share his faith, he never dreamed that sharing a chicken lunch with a Syrian officer would spare the life and ministry of a fellow believer down the road. This is what is meant by living *beyond the limits.* God can use even an ordinary act of providing a chicken lunch to accomplish His will. He can use you if you are willing.

Excerpted from *Living Beyond the Limits* by Franklin Graham (Nashville: Thomas Nelson, Inc., 1998), 79–85. Used by permission.

Y2J Yield to Jesus

If you keep My commandments, you will abide in My love, just as I have kept My Father's commandments and abide in His love. These things I have spoken to you, that My joy may remain in you, and that your joy may be made full. This is My commandment, that you love one another as I have loved you. (John 15:10–12)

Now may the God of hope fill you with all joy and peace in believing, that you may abound in hope by the power of the Holy Spirit. (Rom. 15:13)

READER'S NOTES:

_____

_____

_____

_____

_____

_____

EXAMPLES OF MERCY

Jesus is everything.
—Mother Teresa [Agnes Gonxha Bojaxhia] (1910–1997)
Yugoslavian missionary in India

O n August 31, 1997, Princess Diana died suddenly and tragically. The world suffered another loss the same week—Mother Teresa of Calcutta. While two women could not have been farther apart in socio-economic levels, I believe the world lost two compassionate and merciful women.

One was mourned with fanfare, one without—a reflection of who they were in life. Princess Diana did nothing in secret, while Mother Teresa served her Lord quietly. As different as they were in life, their deaths were grieved on similar levels for the impact their compassion and mercy had on the people who crossed their paths.

I believe Princess Diana's primary concern was for children.

She certainly loved her own sons, but my favorite remembrance of her is the glow of love and compassion captured in photographs when she visited schools, children's hospitals, and war-torn countries where, in April 1999, land mines still killed an average of 60 innocent people a day. She used her available resources to effect change. Her critics probably scoffed at the monies raised from the sale of her clothes and jewels, but she *did* sell them! As beautiful and glamorous as she was, she held material things with an open hand and eliminated the excess of the world's abundance in her life to help ease the suffering of others. While I do not know the root of her motivation, and I have no knowledge that she had a personal relationship with Jesus Christ, we are left with powerful evidence of the fruit that remained.

In contrast, Mother Teresa may not have been high profile by media standards, but at every opportunity she made no secret that she served Jesus Christ. She had no worldly possessions to effect change around her—only her hands-on ministry to those suffering from famine, disease, and poverty. Her hands were wrinkled and her face etched with the lines of compassion, mercy, and care, but she gave of herself with total disregard for any personal loss of comfort or "doing without."

One comment I remember in connection with Mother Teresa is, "She saw the face of Jesus in the faces she ministered to." Do we look for Jesus' face in everyone around us? What an example her life was for us to follow. She saw only Jesus in the people she served. Her only motivation was "*Jesus is everything*." I know that the multitudes to whom she ministered saw Jesus in her.

Everyone in our lives has some physical or emotional need. One vital lesson Princess Diana taught the world is to regard our material blessings and prominent stature in this life as an opportunity to provide for others less fortunate whenever possible.

Mother Teresa's legacy of humility, quietness, and selflessness taught me to look for the face of Jesus in the faces of family, friends, or strangers. My attitude should be one of serving the Lord so that those I serve may see Jesus—the One I serve—in me. *"Jesus is everything."*

> **And I, brethren, when I came to you, did not come with excellence of speech or of wisdom declaring to you the testimony of God. For I determined not to know anything among you except Jesus Christ and Him crucified. I was with you in weakness, in fear, and in much trembling. And my speech and my preaching were not with persuasive words of human wisdom, but in demonstration of the Spirit and of power, that your faith should not be in the wisdom of men but in the power of God. (1 Cor. 2:1–5)**

READER'S NOTES:

_____

_____

_____

_____

_____

_____

A PRAYER FOR TODAY

I have been driven many times upon my knees by the overwhelming conviction that I had nowhere else to go. My own wisdom, and that of all about me, seemed insufficient for that day.

—Abraham Lincoln (1809–65)
16th U.S. President

Pastor Joe Wright of Wichita's Central Christian Church gave the following invocation for the Kansas State Legislature.

Heavenly Father,

We come before you today to ask Your forgiveness and seek Your direction and guidance. We know your Word says, "Woe to those who call evil good," but that is exactly what we have done. We have lost our spiritual equilibrium and inverted our values. We confess that:

We have ridiculed the absolute truth of Your Word and called it pluralism.

We have worshiped other gods and called it multi-culturalism.

We have endorsed perversion and called it an alternative lifestyle.

We have exploited the poor and called it the lottery.

We have neglected the needy and called it self-preservation.

We have rewarded laziness and called it welfare.

We have killed our unborn and called it choice.

We have shot abortionists and called it justifiable.

We have neglected to discipline our children and called it self-esteem.

We have abused power and called it political savvy.

We have coveted our neighbors' possessions and called it ambition.

We have polluted the air with profanity and pornography and called it freedom of expression.

We have ridiculed the time-honored values of our forefathers and called it enlightenment.

Search us, O God, and know our hearts today; cleanse us from every sin, and set us free. Guide and bless these men and women who have been sent here by the people of Kansas, and who have been ordained by You to govern this great state. Grant them the wisdom to rule, and may their decisions direct us to the center of Your will.

I ask it in the name of Your Son, the Living Savior, Jesus Christ. Amen.[6]

For this reason we also, since the day we heard it, do not cease to pray for you, and to ask that you may be filled with the knowledge of His will in all wisdom and

spiritual understanding; that you may walk worthy of the Lord, fully pleasing Him, being fruitful in every good work and increasing in the knowledge of God; strengthened with all might, according to His glorious power, for all patience and longsuffering with joy; giving thanks to the Father who has qualified us to be partakers of the inheritance of the saints in the light. He has delivered us from the power of darkness and conveyed us into the kingdom of the Son of His love, in whom we have redemption through His blood, the forgiveness of sins. (Col. 1:9–14)

READER'S NOTES:

_____

_____

_____

_____

_____

_____

EXTEND A HAND

Make a rule, and pray to God to help you to keep it, never, if possible, to lie down at night without being able to say: "I have made one human being at least a little wiser, or a little happier, or at least a little better this day."

—Charles Kingsley (1819–75)
English clergyman and novelist

BY ROBERT H. SCHULLER

Unfortunately, abandoned children are found all around the world. One of my dearest friends was Bob Pierce. He became a Christian as a young teenager and dedicated his life to being a missionary. He studied, was credentialed, and boarded a boat to China alone to seek his spiritual place in God's good work. Walking on a street, he noticed an American woman holding the hand of a little Chinese child. As Bob and the woman searched each other's eyes, she spoke first: "I can see you're an American. What business are you in?"

"I'm here to be a missionary," he answered naively.

"A missionary?" the rugged lady inquired. "I'm a missionary too, with the Reformed Church. What mission are you with?"

"I'm here praying for guidance," he answered. "I'm looking for my mission. I'm just connected with God."

"Then take this child. He's an orphan. Abandoned. Doesn't belong to anybody. Here! He's yours! Take care of him!" She simply put the boy's little hand in Bob's and left them behind. The world's largest and most respected mission to orphans, refugees, and famine-inflicted nations in the twentieth century was born from that encounter—World Vision. God reached out to an abandoned name-less orphan, using the heart and hand of Bob Pierce. That hurting and homeless child trusted the outstretched hand, and that became the beginning of something awesome! When that child responded with faith and trust, I think the angels in heaven saw a halo glow over Bob Pierce's head.

Another friend of mine, Bill Wilson, was abandoned as a child.

"I was just a little kid when my mom said, 'Let's go for a walk.'" Bill remembers. "She came to a spot in the street and stopped and said, 'Sit here. Don't move. I'll be back.' I waited all day and all night; I slept there on the street. For three days and nights I waited, but she never came back.

"Then a nice man stopped and asked me what I was doing there. I told him and he said, 'Well, come along with me. I'm a Sunday school teacher. Come on. You'll like it. Are you hungry?'

"He fed me and took me to Sunday school, where I heard about God and Jesus. I became a Christian, and I decided I'd spend my life helping abandoned kids."

That's the true story of my friend Bill Wilson, who has organized the largest Sunday school in the world, including the abandoned kids. His school buses pick up children by the thousands, many of them unwanted, and bring them to his mission in the slums of New York—as many as twenty thousand kids gather there every week. Bill still drives one of the buses himself every week he's in town. He drives slowly, his head and eyes shifting sharply and swiftly down the sidewalks and alleys, looking for stray kids.

"You know, Dr. Schuller, who I'm looking for?" Bill asks. "I'm looking for me!"

Bill Wilson has turned his hurt into a halo. So can you!

God is alive, alert, and roaming the streets and alleys of the world. He is living in human beings of all colors, cultures, creeds, and credentials and is reaching out to adopt the spiritual orphans into his family of faith.

Excerpted from *Turning Hurts into Halos* by Robert H. Schuller (Nashville: Thomas Nelson, Inc., 1999), 51–53. Used by permission.

But, beloved, we are confident of better things concerning you, yes, things that accompany salvation, though we speak in this manner. For God is not unjust to forget your work and labor of love which you have shown toward His name, in that you have ministered to the saints, and do minister. And we desire that each one of you show the same diligence to the full assurance of hope until the end . . . This hope we have as an anchor

of the soul, both sure and steadfast, and which enters
the Presence behind the veil. (Heb. 6:9–11, 19)

READER'S NOTES:

_____

_____

_____

_____

_____

_____

I KNOW THIS MUCH TO BE TRUE

Another objection which has been made to this motion is that the Jews look forward to the coming of a great deliverer, to their return to Palestine, to the rebuilding of their temple, to the revival of their ancient worship, and that therefore they will always consider England not their country, but merely as their place of exile . . .

It would be the grossest ignorance of human nature to imagine that the anticipation of an event which is to happen at some time altogether indefinite, . . . which has been *vainly expected during many centuries,* . . . which *even those who confidently expect* that it will happen do not confidently expect that they or their children or their grandchildren will see, can ever occupy the minds of men to a degree as to make them regardless of *what is near and present and certain.*

Indeed, Christians as well as Jews believe that the existing order of things will come to an end. Many Christians believe that Jesus will visibly reign on earth during a thousand years. Expositors of prophecy have gone so far as to fix the year when the millennial period will commence. The prevailing opinion is, I think, *in favor of the year 1866:* but, according to some commentators, *the time is close at hand.*

—Thomas Babington Macaulay
From a speech to Parliament on April 17, 1833
supporting a bill to emancipate Jews in Britain
(emphasis added)

t's amazing that 166 years later, some things haven't changed. The Jews in Britain were emancipated, and some returned to Palestine, but we are still anticipating the "event"—Christ's Second Coming.

We have our own "expositors of prophecy" who have predicted the end of the world. Some of the speculated dates have already passed, just as 1866 passed for those who predicted the world would end then. And many Christians today feel that "the time is close at hand," just as the Christians of Thomas Macaulay's day did.

Is the end of the world near? I don't know. I look forward to Christ's return. Whether it happens in my lifetime or He waits to resurrect me from the grave, my hope in His return is certain. I know this much to be true!

And I feel strongly that early Christians were proactive in their anticipation. We have received warnings that "the existing order of things may come to an end." Certainly this applies to the predicted Y2K crisis, but many have ignored other warnings—situation ethics, moral decay, failing governments, broken families, and so on. Regardless of the calamities we may face in the future, do you have the certainty that you are prepared to meet Christ and live with Him eternally? This is what it means to be prepared. I know this much to be true!

The Parable of the Ten Virgins

Then the kingdom of heaven shall be likened to ten virgins who took their lamps and went out to meet the bridegroom. Now five of them were wise, and five were foolish. Those who were foolish took their lamps and took no oil with them, but the wise took oil in their vessels with their lamps. But while the bridegroom was delayed, they all slumbered and slept. And at midnight a cry was heard: "Behold the bridegroom is coming; go out to meet him!"

Then all those virgins arose and trimmed their lamps. And the foolish said to the wise, "Give us some of your oil, for our lamps are going out." But the wise answered, saying, "No, lest there should not be enough for us and you; but go rather to those who sell, and buy for yourselves."

And while they went to buy, the bridegroom came, and those who were ready went in with him to the wedding; and the door was shut. Afterward the other virgins came also, saying, "Lord, Lord, open to us!" But he answered and said, "Assuredly, I say to you, I do not know you."

Watch therefore, for you know neither the day nor the hour in which the Son of Man is coming." (Matt. 25:1–13, emphasis added)

READER'S NOTES:

_____

_____

_____

_____

_____

_____

Don't Look Back

Occasions of adversity best discover how great virtue or strength each one hath. For occasions do not make a man frail, but show what he is.

—Thomas à Kempis (1380–1471)
German scholar and ecclesiastic

Recently I reread the passage in Genesis 19 on the fate of Sodom and Gomorrah and was struck again by the tragic disobedience of Lot's wife. Everyone knows the story. Because of the Lord's compassion on Lot, his wife was assured of protection and salvation. She, like everyone else, was warned to *not look back* for fear of dire consequences. But she looked anyway.

Have you ever wondered *why* she looked back? Was she just inherently disobedient? Was she curious? Was she concerned about her sons-in-law who were left behind? Was she looking to see if they

84

had changed their minds and decided to follow them? Some commentaries suggest she was too attached to her friends, family, and possessions.

We are told in Genesis 13:11–12 that Lot was wealthy and successful. Perhaps his wife lost her spiritual focus while living a life of material abundance. If God sought to destroy Sodom because of immorality, it is possible that Lot's wife had few days when her thoughts and activities were centered on God. Yet God was willing to let her survive. God knew she was going to look back—why didn't He leave her behind with the sons-in-law who thought the destruction of Sodom and Gomorrah was a joke?

The New King James Version says that Lot "lingered." He was spared because he was hospitable and protected the angels when they entered the city. Was he reluctant to leave behind his wealth, prosperity, and comfort—a life that probably brought him worldly praise from friends and, until now, had brought him security? His lingering provoked the angels to push Lot into action, yelling, "Escape for your life and don't look back!"

The angels physically dragged Lot, his wife, and daughters out of town. Can you picture the women kicking and screaming all the way? I wonder if Lot was whining when he pleaded with the angels not to make him *go all the way to the mountains.* Do you think Lot's wife began to think that there was room for negotiation?

In Luke 17:32 Jesus said, "Remember Lot's wife." Three little words. Can you imagine the image that went through His listeners' minds? Do you think He made His point? Jesus certainly knew why Lot's wife looked back. He didn't entirely clear it up for me, but His point is well taken—the consequences of choosing to "look back."

Do I hold my possessions, family, and friends closer than what He wants me to value most? Regardless of whether we are pre-tribulation, mid-tribulation, or post-tribulation on the time line of Christ's Second Coming and His millennial reign, we should heed God's word to avoid judgment. We cannot become lax or oblivious in the daily activities of our lives.

So many books at the close of the twentieth century speculate that the end of time is at hand. Whether the time is near, our responsibility as believers is to be ready, be watching, and be a testimony to others that a life yielded to Jesus is the only thing that matters.

Unlike Lot's wife, we must look forward and be obedient to God. We must hold on to our possessions and our family with open hands—ready to let go and move ahead to the next step in His plan for us.

> **And as it was in the days of Noah, so it will be also in the days of the Son of Man: They ate, they drank, they were given in marriage, until the day that Noah entered the ark, and the flood came and destroyed them all. Likewise as it was also in the days of Lot: They ate, they drank, they bought, they sold, they planted, they built; but on the day that Lot went out of Sodom it rained fire and brimstone from heaven and destroyed them all. Even so will it be in the day when the Son of Man is revealed. In that day, he who is on the housetop, and his goods are in the house, let him not come down to take them away. And likewise the one who is in the field, let him not turn back. Remember Lot's wife. Whoever**

seeks to save his life will lose it and whoever loses his life will preserve it. I tell you, in that night there will be two men in one bed: the one will be taken and the other will be left. Two women will be grinding together: the one will be taken and the other left. Two men will be in the field: the one will be taken and the other left. (Luke 17: 26–36)

READER'S NOTES:

_____

_____

_____

_____

_____

_____

WHILE I WAS DROWNING

Life, like the waters of the seas, freshens only when it ascends toward heaven.

—Jean Paul Richter (1763–1826)
German humorist

A story that is a matter of public record is told by two officers who survived the Titanic *disaster in a similarly miraculous manner: Colonel Archibald Gracie and Second Officer C.H. Lightoller.*

After valiantly helping to save passengers until they could do nothing else but consider their own fate, Lightoller was near the bridge of the ship, and Gracie was holding onto an iron railing near the highest part of the ship in *Titanic*'s final sinking moments.

Both men knew the water that faced them was 28 degrees—4

degrees below freezing. Lightoller decided to dive headfirst from the bridge and swim toward the crow's nest at water level. Immediately he was sucked against a grating that dragged him down with the ship. He felt certain he would drown and called out to God to give His angels charge over him. Suddenly, Lightoller was blown out of the water by a terrific blast of warm air, long enough to gasp for breath before he went under again. The next rush of air and water landed him alongside an overturned lifeboat that could take him on.

As the ship keeled forward, Gracie successfully avoided a big wave and grabbed hold of the iron railing. The other men who tried to jump the wave were either knocked unconscious or trapped in ropes that dragged them down. Gracie pulled himself onto a high roof and quickly found himself in a swirling whirlpool spiraling down to the ocean floor. He hung on to the railing to a great depth and incredibly still had a sense of direction. Instinctively he knew his life depended on letting go and breaking away from his rapid descent. He pushed off the starboard bow and started swimming away from the doomed ship.

Gracie had no idea how long he was able to hold his breath or how fast he was swimming, but he was numb and swam for quite some time without taking saltwater into his mouth. This fueled his determination to somehow survive. He attributed some buoyancy to his life jacket and the rising air of the sinking ship, but he reached a point when he thought he would have to give up for lack of air.

As he swam below the surface of the water, Gracie was overcome with the certainty that drowning was imminent. He prayed that his spirit would somehow reach the loved ones he was leaving behind with the message, "Good-bye, until we meet again in heaven."

At that moment Colonel Gracie's wife was in New York visiting her sister. Unable to sleep, Mrs. Gracie was nudged by a voice that said, "On your knees and pray." She felt compelled to open her prayer book to the prayer for those at sea and immediately felt that her husband was praying for *her!*

Suddenly the colonel had a second wind and realized he could see the glow of a starry night near the surface and continued ascending. He grabbed onto a wooden crate, and looked around. Other than debris and lifeless bodies, he saw no one and nothing to encourage hope of survival.

He prayed for a rescue boat to pick him up from his meager crate. It seemed unlikely there would be such a boat since he had helped load the last lifeboat at least twenty minutes before he sank down with the *Titanic.*

Moments after praying, Colonel Gracie noticed the last boat he had helped launch, at a considerable distance to his left. It was overturned from the force of the giant wave he had earlier managed to escape. The overturned boat, still afloat, safely held about twelve members of the ship's crew, including Second Officer Lightoller, above the frigid water.

While he was about to drown, Gracie had prayed for his loved ones to be comforted in the knowledge they would one day see him again in heaven. He knew where he would spend eternity. He yielded to the Lord and prepared for what he thought was an inevitable death. Did the Lord spare Gracie and Lightoller in this miraculous manner so they could bear witness to how their lives were saved? Were other lives saved for eternity because of their testimony? I haven't found public record of this, but I like to think that giving the

Lord credit for their safety changed others' lives to focus on an eternal home.

Are you yielded? Are you ready?

There is trouble on the sea; it cannot be quiet. (Jer. 49:23c)

Out of the depths I have cried to You, O Lord;
Lord, hear my voice!
Let Your ears be attentive
To the voice of my supplications. (Ps. 130:1–2)

By awesome deeds in righteousness You will answer us,
O God of our salvation,
You who are the confidence of all the ends of the earth,
And of the far-off seas; . . .
You who still the noise of the seas,
The noise of their waves,
And the tumult of the peoples. (Ps. 65:5, 7)

READER'S NOTES:

_____
_____
_____
_____
_____

SIGNATURE FRAGRANCE

Certainly, virtue is like precious odors, most fragrant
when they are incensed or crushed; for prosperity doth
best discover vice, but adversity doth best discover
virtue.

—Francis Bacon (1561–1626)
English journalist, scientist, author, and philosopher

We all have one—that distinct fragrance or odor that is uniquely
ours. My husband, Boo, and our friend Tom were walking through
a mall together when a woman passed them and Tom asked,
"Wasn't that Beverly's fragrance that just walked by?" I hope that
was a compliment!

I do have a favorite perfume that I wear almost constantly. I
enjoy it thoroughly—isn't that why we choose a fragrance? Using
perfume makes a statement to others around you: "I like this fragrance,

and I hope you like it, too." If a fragrance is recognizable as unique to you, then it becomes your *signature fragrance*.

Do you know God also knows us by our *signature fragrance*? This is not a fragrance we choose from cosmetic counters; it is our fragrance as believers—the one described in the following verses:

> **For we are to God the fragrance of Christ among those who are being saved and among those who are perishing. To the one we are the aroma of death leading to death, and to the other the aroma of life leading to life. And who is sufficient for these things? (2 Cor. 2:15–16)**

> **Therefore be imitators of God as dear children. And walk in love, as Christ also has loved us and given Himself for us, an offering and a sacrifice to God for a sweet-smelling aroma. (Eph. 5:1–2)**

> **I am full, having received from Epaphroditus the things sent from you, a sweet-smelling aroma, an acceptable sacrifice, well pleasing to God. (Phil. 4: 18b)**

It was Roman custom in biblical times for victorious generals to parade through the streets. Their procession included vessels of burning incense, which signified to the spectators a victory for the general and death for the enemy. Now you can understand Paul's meaning of a fragrance that indicates both life and death. To those around us, we can give the fragrance of life in Christ and also be the fragrance of death to those who do not choose Him. This *signature fragrance* definitely takes on new meaning when you think of its effect on others.

We are also commanded to imitate God. How can we even presume to think we *could* imitate God? As earthly parents, we prayerfully desire our children to imitate the good they find in us. As children of God, we can pattern our lives after the certainty of His love for us. If we do so, the Philippians reference to *sweet-smelling aroma* would be the outpouring of His love to us and our giving that love to others. It produces fruit on our account and is an acceptable and pleasing sacrifice to God.

God definitely recognizes the aroma, fragrance, or "odor" of our lives. Each of us is unique and individual with our own "signature." But perhaps the most telling *signature fragrance* to the Lord are the prayers that we offer Him.

In a recent sermon, our pastor referred to Revelation 5:8 and how *all* the prayers of the saints are kept in golden bowls and will be released as incense when the Lamb takes the scroll and releases the seals to complete God's plan for mankind. At the conclusion of the sermon, my husband said the first thing he thought about was the incredible number of "prayers for a parking space" he had offered. That's right—every prayer we have ever prayed will be part of that incense. We laughed at the thought of the "parking space" prayers, but how magnanimous God is to provide my husband with good parking places. *All* our prayers . . . think about it. A mix of ingredients will form the prayer of incense the likes of which we have never known. A priceless fragrance! The *real* "Eternity" fragrance for men and women! A *signature fragrance* unique only to believers and their yielded prayers to the Lord.

Now when He had taken the scroll, the four living creatures and the twenty-four elders fell down before the Lamb, each having a harp, *and golden bowls full of incense, which are all the prayers of the saints.* And they sang a new song, saying:

"You are worthy to take the scroll,

And to open its seals;

For You were slain,

And have redeemed us to God by Your blood

Out of every tribe and tongue and people and nation,

And have made us kings and priests to our God;

And we shall reign on the earth." (Rev. 5:8–10, emphasis added)

READER'S NOTES:

_____

_____

_____

_____

_____

_____

THE LAW OF EMPOWERMENT:
LEADING BY LIFTING UP OTHERS

Example has more followers than reason. We uncon-
sciously imitate what pleases us, and approximate to the
characters we most admire. A generous habit of thought
and action carries with it incalculable influence.

—Christian Nestell Bovee (1820–1904)
American author and editor

BY JOHN C. MAXWELL

O nly secure leaders are able to give themselves away. Mark
Twain once remarked that great things can happen when you don't
care who gets the credit. But you can take that a step further. I
believe the greatest things happen *only* when you give *others* the
credit. That's the Law of Empowerment in action. One-time vice
presidential candidate Admiral James B. Stockdale declared,
"Leadership must be based on goodwill . . . It means obvious and
wholehearted commitment to helping followers . . . What we need

for leaders are men of heart who are so helpful that they, in effect, do away with the need of their jobs. But leaders like that are never out of a job, never out of followers. Strange as it sounds, great leaders gain authority by giving it away."

One of the greatest leaders of this nation was truly gifted at giving his power and authority to others. His name was Abraham Lincoln. The depth of Lincoln's security as a leader can be seen in the selection of his cabinet. Most presidents pick like-minded allies. Not Lincoln. At a time of turmoil for the country, when disparate voices were many, Lincoln brought together a group of leaders who would unify his party and bring strength through diversity and mutual challenge. One Lincoln biographer said this of his method:

> For a president to select a political rival for a cabinet post was not unprecedented; but deliberately to surround himself with all of his disappointed antagonists seemed to be courting disaster. It was a mark of his sincere intentions that Lincoln wanted the advice of men as strong as himself or stronger. That he entertained no fear of being crushed or overridden by such men revealed either surpassing naivete or a tranquil confidence in his powers of leadership.

Lincoln lived the Law of Empowerment. His security enabled him to give his power away.

Finding strong leaders to empower. Lincoln's ability to empower played a major role in his relationship with his generals during the Civil War. In the beginning, he had trouble finding worthy recipients of his confidence. When the Southern states seceded, the finest generals in the land went south to serve the Confederacy. But Lincoln never lost hope, nor did he neglect to give his leaders power and freedom, even when that strategy failed with previous generals.

For example, in June of 1863, Lincoln put the command of the Army of the Potomac into the hands of General George G. Meade. Lincoln hoped that he would do a better job than had preceding generals Ambrose E. Burnside and Joseph Hooker. Within hours of Meade's appointment, Lincoln sent a courier to him. The president's message, in part, said,

> Considering the circumstances, no one ever received a more important command; and I cannot doubt that you will fully justify the confidence which the Government has reposed in you. You will not be hampered by any minute instructions from these headquarters. Your army is free to act as you may deem proper under the circumstances as they arise . . . All forces within the sphere of your operations will be held subject to your orders.

As it turned out, Meade's first significant challenge came as he commanded the army at a small Pennsylvania town named Gettysburg. It was a test he passed with authority. In the end, though, Meade was not the general who would make full use of the power Lincoln offered. It took Ulysses S. Grant to turn the war around. But Meade stopped General Robert E. Lee's army when it counted, and he prevented the Confederacy from moving on Washington.

Lincoln's use of the Law of Empowerment was consistent. Even when his generals performed poorly, Lincoln took the blame. Lincoln expert Donald T. Phillips acknowledged, "Throughout the war Lincoln continued to accept public responsibility for battles lost or opportunities missed." Lincoln was able to stand strongly during the war and continually give power to others because of his rock-solid security.

The power of empowerment. A key to empowering others is a high belief in people. I feel I've been fortunate because believing in others has always been very easy for me. I recently received a note from the one person, outside my family, whom I have worked hardest to empower. His name is Dan Reiland. He was my executive pastor when I was at Skyline, and today he is the vice president for leadership development at INJOY. Dan wrote,

> John,
>
> The ultimate in mentoring has come to pass. I am being asked to teach on the topic of empowerment! I can do this only because you first empowered me. The day is still crystal clear in my mind when you took a risk and chose me as your Executive Pastor. You trusted me with significant responsibility, the day-to-day leadership of the staff and ministries of your church. You released me with authority . . . You believed in me—perhaps more than I believed in myself. You demonstrated your faith and confidence in me is such a way that I could tap into your belief, and eventually it became my own.
>
> I am so very grateful for your life-changing impact on my life. Saying thank you hardly touches it. "I love and appreciate you" is better. Perhaps the best way I can show my gratitude is to pass on the gift you have given me to other leaders in my life.
>
> Dan

I am grateful to Dan for all he has done for me, and I believe he has returned to me much more than I have given to him. And I've genuinely enjoyed the time I've spent with Dan helping him grow. The truth is that empowerment is powerful—not only for the person being developed, but also for the mentor. Enlarging others makes you larger. Dan has made me better than I am, not just because he helped me achieve much more than I could have done on my own, but also because the whole process made me a better leader. That is the impact of the Law of Empowerment.

Excerpted from *The 21 Irrefutable Laws of Leadership* by John C. Maxwell (Nashville: Thomas Nelson, Inc., 1998), 127–31. Used by permission.

Be kindly affectionate to one another with brotherly love, in honor giving preference to one another; not lagging in diligence, fervent in spirit, serving the Lord; rejoicing in hope, patient in tribulation, continuing steadfastly in prayer; distributing to the needs of the saints, given to hospitality. Bless those who persecute you; bless and do not curse. Rejoice with those who rejoice and weep with those who weep. Be of the same mind toward one another. Do not set your mind on high things but associate with the humble. Do not be wise in your own opinion. (Rom. 12:10–16)

READER'S NOTES:

_____

_____

CAUTION LIGHTS

No man may safely rule but he that hath learned gladly to
obey.

—Thomas à Kempis (1380–1471)
German scholar and ecclesiastic

Do you ignore yellow traffic lights? Some traffic schools teach
us to yield at a yellow light. What about flashing lights of caution?
Do you slow down at caution lights? Sometimes I think it is an
unwritten rule of the road for drivers—in Dallas anyway—that a
yellow light means "step on the gas" and a red light means "stop if
you must."

In 1998 President Clinton addressed a room full of clergy in the
White House prior to a prayer breakfast. Since the event was televised, the nation was privy to his words, and I was watching. The
president was expected to make a statement regarding his "plan of

repentance" for his public moral failure. The speech was what I expected, but Mr. Clinton made an interesting comment that I thought meritorious. He told the nation that he planned to be accountable and he had a list of "caution lights" to heed in his life.

Caution lights. As they pertain to traffic lights, we know we should slow down and yield. So why don't we? As they pertain to Mr. Clinton's plan for his life, I pray he will see his "caution lights" and yield to them. As they pertain to us, what are the things we should recognize as caution lights, those things that might keep us from yielding to Jesus? I often wish that all the lights in my life were as easily recognized as a yellow light or a brightly colored yield sign. Something which may seem innocent in a Christian's life may actually be a caution light, even those things we see as positives. Let me share some examples.

Money is not a sin, but it should be considered a caution light. Success is not a sin, but it should be considered a caution light. The same holds true for position, power, security, and comfort; while they are attributes we desire, they become caution lights when we focus solely on them.

Of course there are more obvious caution lights—the words we use, looking out for "number one," and selfish ambition are all cautions. What are our minds dwelling on? Our thoughts should be on things that are true, noble, just, pure, lovely, of good report, of virtue, and praiseworthy.

Covetousness and jealousy are bright caution lights. We often let our envy of another's good fortune become our misfortune. Jesus warned us about covetousness in Luke 12:15: "Take heed and beware of covetousness, for one's life does not consist in the abundance of the things he possesses." When we begin counting our material wealth—our "abundance of things"—we find a definite caution light.

What are the caution lights in your life? Are your circumstances, your attitudes, your actions, or your relationships hindering you from a life yielded to Jesus? Do you yield to the caution lights in your life, or do you step on the gas to ignore them any way you can?

Watch, stand fast in the faith, be brave, be strong. (1 Cor. 16:13)

READER'S NOTES:

_____

_____

_____

_____

_____

_____

Victory over Prayerlessness

> Prayer is a sincere, sensible, affectionate pouring out of
> the soul to God, through Christ, in the strength and assis-
> tance of the Spirit, for such things as God has promised.
> —John Bunyan (1628–88)
> English religious author

BY BECKY TIRABASSI

I've always enjoyed a convention to get out of a spiritual lull.
Speakers, singing, challenge. And if there ever was a time in my life
when I needed a lift or renewal, it was now! Before leaving
Cleveland for the fortieth anniversary of the Youth For Christ convention in Chicago, I came to the conclusion that my spiritual
drought was the result of burnout—overwork, little rest, and too
much responsibility. Therefore, I purposed in my mind to quit the
ministry. It seemed an appropriate time to leave the working world,
relax, omit outside stress, and just be happy *inside*.

But listening to the first speaker at the convention, I was shocked by his comment: "If you think it's time to quit, it's too soon!" This happened to me before. Through one person, God was speaking to me, as if I were the only person in the room.

The words from that sentence resounded and echoed in my ears until I acknowledged that they were directly from God to me. God seemed to be saying, "Don't get up. Don't go anywhere. Don't day-dream or pretend you don't hear My voice. You've been looking for answers, and I'm going to give them to you . . . though not what you might expect."

Sandwiched between perfect strangers, I didn't dare move. Without a friend to explain my experience to, I sat back, exhaled, and took the slow, deep breath of a person curious with anticipation. Though somewhat afraid of what God might say or do, I nervously awaited something unusual or supernatural to occur.

Then it unfolded, on cue, but without rehearsal. Each keynote speaker had been asked to speak on how God had been at work in the Youth For Christ organization during the previous forty years. Though none of them were given a more specific theme, there was one unexpected thread—especially for my ears—prayer.

Prayer? If the convention had been promoted as a prayer conference, I would have never considered attending. Not that I didn't believe in prayer and its value for the Christian. I just had not, up to that point in time, considered prayer an instrumental part of my daily walk with Christ. Oh, I prayed. I kept a journal of written conversations with the Lord. When in distress or trouble, I regularly released an "I need help" prayer. I often found myself asking God for a parking space close to a store entrance during a thunderstorm or snowstorm, but sadly, that was the extent of prayer in my Christian life.

Certainly young, busy Christians shouldn't be expected to carry on with such a serious (and boring) discipline, should they? Prayer, to be perfectly honest, was not a priority—though it was a principle I believed in and encouraged others to do the same.

Like a bombshell, the message hit with the second speaker. Even as he began to share, his sincerity about God, ministry, and prayer became evident. He told of regular, daily intercession for the salvation of his neighbors. I was struck with the thought of his incredibly busy schedule and amazed that he made time to pray for his neighbors. I didn't even know my neighbors' names!

As he continued, his tone of voice rose, and his intensity flared as he pounded out the words of James 4:2. Looking at those of us who needed to call on God's power most and probably used it least, he cried, "You do not have because you do not ask!" (James 4:2). I actually opened my Bible to the verse, thinking that it couldn't really say that—at least, not in that way. It wasn't that blatant, was it? Then he choked up with tears and proceeded to impress upon the listeners the fervency of his message: "Prayerlessness, for the believer, is sin."

How he phrased it, said it, or convinced me, I'm still unsure, but the Holy Spirit began His own conviction on Saturday morning. I cried in silent shame and humiliation through every general session because of my lack of prayer, as each godly speaker related tremendous miracles of healing, incredible circumstances of God's intervention, and even the harvest of souls saved years later *due to daily, consistent prayer.*

Their stories magnified and illuminated the self-sufficient approach to ministry and daily Christian life that I was living because of my prayerlessness. By then, only one word aptly described my state: *ashamed*. I was ashamed of myself for the audacity to lead Bible studies, evangelize, and work for God daily, but spend no personal time with Him in prayer, in conversation, or even in confession.

As the weekend came to a close, we were invited to choose from a list of various optional seminars. A workshop on prayer flashed like a neon light from my pamphlet. That was my choice.

As my good friend and I were standing at the entrance to this workshop, laughter seemed an appropriate reaction to my desire to attend a workshop on prayer. Both of us felt the discipline of prayer was an extremely serious matter, but neither of us did anything that was serious (at least up to that point in time).

Parting ways, I slowly entered the workshop, feeling awkward and hesitant. I picked a seat in the back of the auditorium thinking I might leave the room if it got too uncomfortable.

Once again, tears flowed uncontrollably down my cheeks throughout the hour presentation on prayer as the speaker talked of the power available to a believer who prays. To make matters worse, no one else in the room seemed to react to the speaker with similar emotion, and my blubbering appeared out of place. I just couldn't pinpoint the root of all of this!

But God's work was being completed within me. Through the weekend and culminating with this workshop, I was indeed convinced that prayerlessness was sin. If I truly believed that spending time with God in prayer was actually engaging in conversation with my Creator, Friend, Savior, Leader, and King, why did I overlook, avoid, forget, or fall asleep in the middle of prayers? If I truly wanted to be used by God to evangelize and disciple the world for Christ, why did I place so little emphasis on time alone with Him?

My perspective on prayer was changing.

I sat frozen as all three hundred workshop attendees filed out of the room. I was probably an interesting sight with streaked makeup and red puffy cheeks. I just didn't want to leave the room without making dramatic changes in my life, but where to start and how to maintain them seemed beyond my grasp. Then a woman touched my shoulder, offering to pray with me.

I bowed my head, determined to make a lifelong decision to change. But change what? Change how? The words of prayer flowed from my mouth with the same intensity and mystery as my initial prayer for salvation came so desperately seven years earlier. Without premeditation, I made a decision in front of God and another person to pray for an hour a day for the rest of my life!

I knew myself too well. If I had given a trial period to see if "I liked it" or if "it fit into my busy life," I would have allowed my decision to fizzle into a sweet memory as a "too difficult for me" discipline.

But I sensed God's presence and provision in this decision, and I weighed the benefits of prayer in a believer's life versus life without it all week long. It was a hands-down decision to pursue the discipline.

Mentally drifting back to the seminar, I remembered a number of verses and principles about prayer the speaker had explained. Not a single verse had been new—Matthew 6:31–34 and Philippians 4:6–7, 19—yet for the first time, those words were alive and fresh and inviting. Their practicality pierced me as I mentally walked with them through a typical day. As I toyed with actually believing them, they stunned me with their power.

An hour a day. I had to take a radical step closer to God. I took the plunge and left that room bathed afresh in the power of the

Holy Spirit. It was all I could do to find Kinney, my friend, go to lunch, and pour out to her all that I felt God was saying to me. Something was coming alive within me. The relationship with God I experienced as a young, "on fire," baby Christian was aglow. That dependency, that willingness to be guided by God, to listen to Him, to share every thought with Him, was reignited within me as acceptable, not as childish. With the true style of an evangelist, I elaborated on all that I heard and all that God was going to do in my life because of prayer. We laughed, we cried, and both of us thought how special this convention had been—certain God had touched our lives.

It was to be beyond my wildest expectations what power God would release into my life from that day forward because of prayer, but first, I had to master the discipline. O. Hallesby, author of *Prayer*, profoundly submits that "nothing so furthers our prayer life as the feeling of our own helplessness." This admission—or concession—offers great hope to those of us discouraged with our self-effort and continuous lack of victory in the pursuit of a true and fulfilling prayer life.

Andrew Murray in his classic, *The Prayer Life*, discusses prayerlessness in the life of a believer, even and especially the minister, at great length. He concludes, "If we recognize, in the first place, that a right relationship with the Lord Jesus Christ, above all else, *includes prayer*, according to God's will, then we have something which gives us the right to rejoice in Him and to rest in Him."

Excerpt from *Let Prayer Change Your Life Workbook* by Becky Tirabassi (Nashville: Thomas Nelson, Inc., 1995), 3–9. Used by permission.

Come and hear, all you who fear God,
And I will declare what He has done for my soul.
I cried to Him with my mouth,
And He was extolled with my tongue.
If I regard iniquity in my heart,
The Lord will not hear.
But certainly God has heard me;
He has attended to the voice of my prayer.
Blessed be God,
Who has not turned away my prayer,
Nor His mercy from me! (Ps. 66:16–20)

READER'S NOTES:

_____
_____
_____
_____
_____
_____

KEEP YOUR FOCUS

My will is weak, my strength is frail, and all my hope is
nearly gone; I can but trust thy working true to gently
hold and lead me on.

—Watchman Nee (1903–72)
Chinese author and preacher

BY MICHAEL W. SMITH

Back in science class, I learned that you could use a magnifying
glass on a sunny day to create enough heat to burn a hole in paper.
The key was concentrating all the energy on a single point.

In *The Message,* Eugene Peterson came up with a great way to
express the Christian's response to this principle in Hebrews 12:

Keep your eyes on Jesus, who both began and finished
this race we're in. Study how he did it. Because he never
lost sight of where he was headed—that exhilarating

111

finish in and with God—he could put up with anything along the way: cross, shame, whatever. And now he's there, in the place of honor, right alongside God. When you find yourselves lagging in your faith, go over that story again, item by item, that long litany of hostility he plowed through. That will shoot adrenaline into your souls! (Heb. 12:2–3, The Message)

It's easy to get distracted. We're like Martha when Jesus came to visit. She busily tried to be a good hostess while her sister, Mary, listened at Jesus' feet. When she finally asked the Lord to make Mary help her, Jesus replied, "Martha, Martha, you are worried and troubled about many things. But one thing is needed, and Mary has chosen that good part, which will not be taken away from her." (Luke 10:41b–42, The Message)

My updated translation is this: "Slow down, Martha. You're running around like a maniac. Sit down and listen. You're missing out on what matters here." I need to hear those words, and maybe you do too.

Occasionally, I have so much on my schedule that I'm basically out of control. I can't concentrate on what's before me because I'm thinking about what I just finished and what lies ahead. It's a pretty crazy way to live—and when things get like that, I just lose it.

I find myself wanting to escape to my favorite hideaway in Colorado where I can spend time in solitude and get with God. I feel like a wrung-out sponge, dry and crushed, and I desperately need the Father to pour out His peace and joy on me to fill me up again.

Sometimes I can work Colorado into my schedule; other times I try to experience personal revival by driving in the country or walking around the farm. In those times of solitude God puts my priorities back in order, He reminds me of my purpose, and refuels me with what I need to follow Him with passion.

Excerpted from *Your Place in This World,* by Michael W. Smith (Nashville: Thomas Nelson, Inc., 1998), 124–126. Used by permission.

Looking unto Jesus, the author and finisher of our faith, who for the joy that was set before Him endured the cross, despising the shame, and has sat down at the right hand of the throne of God. For consider Him who endured such hostility from sinners against Himself, lest you become weary and discouraged in your souls. (Heb. 12:2–3)

READER'S NOTES:

_____

_____

_____

_____

_____

_____

IS JESUS WORTH IT ALL?

Every step toward Christ kills a doubt. Every thought, word, and deed for Him carries you away from discouragement.

—T.L. Cuyler (1822–1909)
American clergyman

BY SHEILA WALSH

*J*ob's predicament. The Lord gave Satan permission to tear Job's life apart. But true to God's prediction, Job stood fast. In the midst of his sorrow, Job declared, "The Lord gave and the Lord has taken away. Blessed be the name of the Lord" (Job 1:21).

Not long afterward, God and Satan met again, and the Lord said, "Well, what do you think about Job now? Didn't I tell you there was nobody on earth like him? He was ruined for no reason, but he only praised My Name and continues to be without blame."

Satan sneered and retorted with a proverb often used by tradesmen of Job's time: "One skin for another! Of course, Job was willing to give up the lives of his animals, his servants, and his children, *but what about his own skin?* Every human is selfish. Why don't you let me touch Job's body and ruin his health? A man can live without his children. A man can live without his wealth, but cause him personal pain, and he'll curse You to Your face!"

"All right then," God replied. "Touch Job's body, but you cannot kill him."

And so Satan afflicted Job from the top of his head to the bottom of his feet with the most painful kinds of boils and sores. In incredible misery, Job sat on a heap of ashes, scraping his sores with a piece of broken pottery, but he never said a word against God.

What does Job's story have to say to you and me? Is it a dangerous thing to fall into the hands of God? Can He be trusted? What does it really mean to be His servant and His child? Why would God stand back and allow our mortal enemy to toy with us?

I've often wondered how Job prayed during those seven days and seven nights when the sky was like brass and nobody seemed to be listening. I wonder whether Job might at least have been tempted to mutter, *Lord, it wasn't supposed to be this way.*

No, a lot of life isn't supposed to be this way, but it is. And when our prayers bounce off the ceiling and land right back in our faces, we feel guilty for asking why. After all, Christians are supposed to have all the answers. Theoretically, we are the ones who can deal with life because we have a powerful and loving God who hears our prayers and gives the victory. In reality, God often seems to respond with a "No," or a "Please wait. My plan is in place; just trust Me."

I believe that when we base our faith on apparent answered

prayer, getting the solutions to our problems *right now,* we're in real trouble. If we mistake God's silence for indifference, we are miserable people. If we give up when we no longer understand, we reject His caring, steadfast love and cut ourselves off from our only real hope.

Satan, of course, is sitting back hoping that's exactly what will happen—that we will give up, quit, and pack it in. That's why Satan slithered up to a sixty-year-old heartbroken man whose wife had just left him after he tried to be honest. Satan said to him, "You were better off before you met God. You still had your wife then."

And that's why Satan crawled under the bridge to tell a lonely young boy, "You're forgotten. You're nobody. Why don't you end it all?"

Satan specializes in lies, confusion, desperation, and depression. As a fallen angel, he is a limited being, but he still has tremendous powers and the most clever strategies. He moves in to tempt us at our particular weakness, and he always times his temptations to come when we're feeling stressed, desperate, and confused. He throws his worst in our faces and then sits back to see what will happen.

We often ask, "Can I really trust God? Where is He? Why isn't He riding to the rescue?" Perhaps the real question is, "Can God trust *me?*"

Is Jesus worth it all? If I say I'm willing to follow Jesus, what do I mean? I believe there is only one valid reason for following Jesus: because He is worth it. He *is* worth it—His love, His understanding, His compassion—because of who He is. I follow Him with no strings attached, not telling God that I'll do this if He'll come through with that. Either Jesus is worth it only because He is Jesus, or He is worth nothing.

Turning point. When life doesn't make sense anymore, we can give up, or we can remember who Jesus really is and that no matter how dark it gets, He is worth it all.

Excerpted from *Life Is Tough but God Is Faithful* by Sheila Walsh (Nashville: Thomas Nelson, Inc., 1999), 17–20. Used by permission.

> **Therefore, since all these things will be dissolved, what manner of persons ought you to be in holy conduct and godliness, looking for and hastening the coming of the day of the God, because of which the heavens will be dissolved, being on fire, and the elements will melt with fervent heat? Nevertheless we, according to His promise, look for new heavens and a new earth in which righteousness dwells. (2 Peter 3: 11–13)**

READER'S NOTES:

_____

_____

_____

_____

_____

_____

THE COURAGE TO CONFRONT

Christianity is not a theory or speculation, but a life; not
a philosophy of life, but a life and a living process.
—Samuel Taylor Coleridge (1772–1834)
English poet and critic

BY FRANKLIN GRAHAM

You call yourself a Christian? For the past fifteen years, Dennis
[Agajanian] and I have participated in a charity event known as the
Colorado 500, a motorcycle ride that supports local hospitals and
schools. It can sometimes appear to be the who's who of the racing
circuit, with some of the most famous drivers in the world participating. At least 300 dirt bikes cross a single-track trail through narrow mountain passes and over the rugged Colorado terrain.

The day before the ride, Dennis and I were adjusting the fuel/air
mixtures in our carburetors to prepare them for high altitude. We
were trying to hurry so that we could test-ride our bikes later that day.

A man and woman pulled a white trailer up next to where we were working. The woman was one of those bubbly, vivacious types—overly friendly. She was attractive, with sandy hair and blue eyes. As Dennis and I fine-tuned our bikes, she came down the steps of the RV and introduced herself. In the course of the conversation, she mentioned that she was a Christian. She hung around for a while, asking a lot of questions.

Her actions made me a little nervous, so I excused myself. "Dennis, I'll be back in a couple of hours. We'll test the bikes then." I headed to the Aspen Airport to meet a friend and fellow motorcycle rider, Pete Robinson.

When I got back to the ranch, I found Dennis's face red and the woman's eyes bloodshot. The man who was with the young woman didn't look too happy either. In fact, he looked like he wanted to kill someone. I approached with a bit of caution.

"Dennis," I pulled him aside, "I've only been gone an hour and a half, and it looks like you've got everybody hoppin' mad about something. What's goin' on?"

"That woman," Dennis answered pointing, "told me she's heard me play and loves my music. She's been hanging around ever since you left."

"Say what?" I looked at him, puzzled. "Why is that a problem?"

Dennis told me what had transpired after I had left. The guy she was staying with had stepped out of the trailer. He was much older. She quickly introduced him to Dennis, but Dennis began to sense their relationship wasn't what it ought to be. Maybe it was the guilty look on the guy's face.

"Is this your husband?" Dennis quizzed.

"No."

"Okay," Dennis paused. "Who is he?"

"My boyfriend."

"Boyfriend?"

"Mmmhmm."

"And this is your camper here?"

"No, it's his."

"His, huh? So are you driving back to Denver tonight?"

"No."

"You're going to stay with him?"

"Yeah."

"And you call yourself a Christian?"

"Well, sure."

Dennis had looked this girl straight in the eyes and said, "Don't you know this is wrong? This is a sin against God. Don't do this."

The woman stuttered. Dennis didn't let up. "God loves you. You can't stay with him. It's sin and you know it."

She had finally turned away in tears. Dennis didn't know what to do. He can't stand to see a girl cry. He bent down to check the air pressure in his bike's tires. When he looked over his shoulder, she was still crying.

Dennis said with a hint of compassion, "In spite of what you do, God loves you and wants to forgive you. When you look into your boyfriend's eyes tonight, remember that you are hurting the heart of God."

That's when I pulled up.

After hearing Dennis's story, I couldn't help but admire his honesty and, yes, his fearlessness. Dennis had confronted this young woman head-on. He didn't enjoy doing it; in fact, he was rather uneasy about the whole incident, but he believed (and rightly so) that if she wanted to call herself a Christian and a follower of Jesus Christ, then she ought to live like one by obeying God's Word, which says, "Get rid of all moral filth and the evil that is so prevalent and humbly accept the word planted in you" (James 1:21 NIV).

The next day, Wally Dallenbach, the host for this charity event, and his wife, Peppy, asked Dennis to play a few songs and me to say a few words and pray before the ride got started. After Dennis sang, he stood at the back of the crowd. He noticed the young woman there. Dennis doesn't do well disguising his feelings. What you see is what you get. He can't pull the shade on sin and pretend it isn't there.

The woman discreetly eyed Dennis with a somewhat forlorn look. Dennis stared back, determined to give the Holy Spirit a little help. He pointed to her and mouthed the words *God loves you*. She started to cry. The boyfriend glared back at Dennis with malice. He was well aware of what was going on, but a man his age and size was no match for Dennis, so he had no choice but to keep his distance.

After I finished praying, all the guys headed for their bikes and began putting on their gear. Three hundred dirt bikes revved up in unison and spewed their exhaust into the air. The noise was deafening, like a million hornets surrounded us.

Within seconds, the Colorado 500 was underway and our concentration was refocused on keeping our wheels on course.

I never saw that woman again, but Dennis did.

Bold living. What I appreciate about Dennis is that he didn't allow a woman's flattery to influence his convictions. Some people might think Dennis should have been less direct, but our fear of offending others can have grave eternal consequences.

The fact is, if we want to make a difference in the kingdom of God, at times we must act with uncompromising boldness and live it as well. As an evangelist, I preach openly against sin—and that's not too fashionable these days. Many would argue that it simply isn't politically correct, but God says in Ezekiel:

> **I have made you a watchman . . . therefore you shall hear a word from My mouth and warn them for Me. When I say to the wicked, "O wicked man, you shall surely die!" and you do not speak to warn the wicked from his way, that wicked man shall die in his iniquity; but his blood I will require at your hand. (Ezek. 33:7–8)**

Dennis confronted this woman in the footsteps of the Old Testament prophet Ezekiel, whose name means "strengthened by God." Dennis didn't let his fan's admiration or the boyfriend's angry reaction deter him from speaking out against sin. Dennis simply spoke the truth, and the truth, as we'll see, eventually set that woman free.

Do you remember me? About two years after Dennis confronted the young woman at the Colorado 500, he was playing at a church in Denver. After the concert, a woman came up to him and asked, "Do you remember me?"

"No, I'm sorry I don't," Dennis confessed.

"Two years ago, I was at the Colorado 500, living in sin with a man, and you rebuked me. Remember?"

Dennis swallowed hard, ready for a confrontation.

"I was afraid to give up my relationship for fear of being alone," the woman continued, much to Dennis's surprise. "I went home after the event and asked God to forgive me. I want you to know that today I'm happily married and a new mother. You cared enough to speak the truth, not just what I wanted to hear. Thank you for helping me get my life right with the Lord. I couldn't be happier."

When Dennis and I return each year for the Colorado 500, we think of that young lady and rejoice that her life is changed. To live a life beyond the limits, we must learn to be courageous when dealing with those who are steeped in worldly lifestyles. Once we're fine tuned this way, there are *no limits* to how God can use us. This is a promise: "Be strong and very courageous. Be careful to obey all the law . . . do not turn from it to the right or to the left, that you may be successful wherever you go" (Josh. 1:7 NIV).

Excerpted from *Living Beyond the Limits* by Franklin Graham (Nashville: Thomas Nelson, Inc., 1998), 25–29, 31–32. Used by permission.

Only be strong and very courageous, that you may observe to do according to all the law which Moses My servant commanded you; do not turn from it to the right hand or to the left, that you may prosper wherever you go. This Book of the Law shall not depart from your mouth, but you shall meditate in it day and night, that you may observe to do according to all that is written in it. For then you will make your way prosperous, and then you will have good success. Have I not commanded

you? Be strong and of good courage; do not be afraid,
nor be dismayed, for the Lord your God is with you
wherever you go. (Josh. 1: 7–9)

READER'S NOTES:

_____

_____

_____

_____

_____

_____

PROGRESSING PILGRIMS

Confession of sin comes from the offer of mercy . . .
Mercy displayed causes confession to flow, and confession flowing opens the way for mercy. If I have not a contrite heart, God's mercy will never be mine; but if God
had not manifested his mercy in Christ, I could never
have had a contrite heart.

—Neil Arnot (1788–1874)
Scottish physician

Who was John Bunyan? You may recognize him as the author of *A Pilgrim's Progress*, an allegorical children's story of a man named Christian and his pilgrimage as a Christian walking with God in this world toward his final destination, "the Celestial City." You may know Bunyan by this book; however, it is only one of sixty books he wrote while he lived his sixty years on earth. So, who was John Bunyan?

John Bunyan belongs in a book about yielding to Jesus. More than three hundred years after *A Pilgrim's Progress* was authored, it is still being read, sometimes more than once. It is more than a Christian classic—*immortal* might be a more fitting word, certainly *eternal*. But who was this man?

As a boy John searched for peace in his heart. His father was a poor tinker, a mender of pots and pans. He spent Sundays in church with his English Puritan family. He lived during the time of King Charles, the Dissenters, and the Reformation movement. While many other Puritan pilgrims made their way to the "New World," John's family stayed in England. Two experiences in John's youth left him questioning whether he would go to heaven: a couple who was hanged for past crimes, and the death of his mother. In both instances John was assured by his family that he could get to heaven. John knew Jesus died for his sins and that God would forgive him, but still John was uncertain—too much confusion for a little boy.

John worked alongside his father until he could become a soldier and fight during the English Civil War. Once he became a soldier, he was more lost and confused than before. He spent most of his free time reading in bookshops near his post. Since most other soldiers could not read, this activity served to isolate him even more. The soldiers were commanded to attend church services which John dreaded attending.

But one night he met Mary, the girl who would eventually become his wife. During this time, John was serving a month of guard duty. One night he wanted to see Mary; it was her birthday, and his friend, Fred, offered to stand guard in his place. That night Royalists raided John's post. While quite a few of the Royalist soldiers were killed, only one Parliamentary guard was lost: John's friend. Imagine John's anguish. Fred was killed in his place.

John was wracked with grief. He felt certain he would be dead if not for his friend. John's commander agreed this might be true and felt moved to point out to John that Jesus Christ also died in John's place but as His Savior.

Before his death, Fred had also talked to John about Jesus many times. At his commander's words John was reminded of this. He thought, *Fred often talked about Him. I have wanted to serve Him, too, but I am so wicked of heart. I'm trying to break off sinning, and I mean to serve Him.*

The commander added that he would pray for John and remarked that John's life must have been spared because God had some work for him to do.

But, things didn't happen very fast. John was mustered out of the army with a month's pay when the course of the war changed. He was twenty-one years old and still on an aimless path. When he returned home, he became a tinker like his father and eventually wed his bride-to-be, Mary.

Mary knew John misspent his free time drinking, and she told him she didn't want a drunkard for a husband. In the evenings she would read to John from the only two books she had brought from her father's house: *The Plain Man's Path to Heaven* and *The Practice of Piety*. She hoped John would become more like the godly man her father was. A woman rebuked John publicly for swearing and, by the work of God, he stopped. John tried to reform himself in other ways. He stopped drinking, worked hard, went to church every Sunday, and spent less time with his game-playing friends.

One afternoon while playing ball with his friends, John heard a voice: "John Bunyan, wilt thou leave thy sins and go to heaven, or keep them and go to hell?" He was overcome by the directness of the voice, but dismissed it, saying, "I'm damned anyhow, so I might as well enjoy my sins." John was still consumed with thoughts of a wrathful God.

Shortly after John's encounter, havoc reigned in England, and the monarchy was overthrown. During this confusing time, Mary became pregnant. She pleaded with John to come to know Jesus as his Savior; he felt the same sense of urgency. Mary assured him once more, "All you have to do is trust him, John. He will save you."

Nine months later their baby girl was born—blind. In his search for understanding, John overheard some nuns talking about God's love and man's emptiness without Him. Days later, John approached the women with the question: "Do you think I could have the new birth?"

The women, members of St. Johns church, invited John to attend Sunday services, and the pastor took special care with him. In the meantime, John began to read the story of Martin Luther. Realizing that Luther's journey was similar to his own, John found hope that he might indeed be saved. And one night, alone in the attic room of his home, John prayed, "I can but die, and if I must die, then I shall die lying at the feet of Jesus, trusting Him for His mercy."

John, assured of his salvation, shared the news with Mary and began the rest of his life—preaching. Though he was never "ordained" and had little education, Jesus was enough. As a test to his new-found faith, Mary died when their firstborn child was eight years old, leaving behind four children. In his faithfulness, John was blessed with another godly wife, Bitsy, who was at his side until the day he died.

John was imprisoned three times for proclaiming his Christianity. During his twelve years in jail, he continued putting pen to paper. Bitsy and his children visited him regularly and brought him food and other necessities. Sometimes he wrote on the food sacks and other scraps of paper, anything he could share the Word on. Many of his writings were publicly banned, but he kept persisting.

During his third and shortest prison term, John got the idea to write down the children's story he had been telling his family for years. The book was almost completed when he was pardoned, and upon his release he finished the 250-page book he called *A Pilgrim's Progress*.

To circumvent the board of censors who oversaw the publication of printed literature, the publisher did not tell the board John was the author. *Progress* was received with overwhelming praise.

The rest, as they say, is history. John Bunyan was fifty years old when *A Pilgrim's Progress* was released. The first month it sold more than 100,000 copies and was constantly reprinted. John saw eleven editions of the book printed in his lifetime, and he wrote six more books during his final ten years. His last words as he looked toward heaven were of assurance, "Take me, for I come to Thee." He finally knew the peace he'd longed for.

So, who was John Bunyan? A sinner, like you and me. Forgiven, like you and me. Yielded, just as we should be—*pilgrims progressing* toward "the Celestial City."

But what does it say? *"The word is near you, in your mouth and in your heart"* (that is, the word of faith which we preach): that if you confess with your mouth the Lord

Jesus and believe in your heart that God has raised Him from the dead, you will be saved. For with the heart one believes unto righteousness, and with the mouth confession is made unto salvation. For the Scripture says, *"Whoever believes on Him will not be put to shame."* For there is no distinction between Jew and Greek, for the same Lord over all is rich to all who call upon Him. For *"whoever calls on the name of the Lord shall be saved."* (Rom. 10:8–13, emphasis added)

READER'S NOTES:

_____

_____

_____

_____

_____

_____

CHANNEL MARKERS

████████████████████████████████████

> The highest obedience in the spiritual life is to be able always, and in all things to say, "Not my will, but thine be done."
>
> —Tryon Edwards (1809–94)
> American theologian and editor

BY CHARLES STANLEY

Let's look at how to discover God's will. First, why do we even have to discover God's will? If I am His child and He is my heavenly Father, why doesn't He just make it plain? Why all the seeming mystery? Why all the tension? Why all the pressure? Why all the tears and the fasting and the praying?

The answer to that question lies behind this whole issue of knowing God's will. As you read the New Testament and the Old Testament, you find that God is always more interested in revealing Himself than simply revealing details about His will for us. God does not want to function simply as an information center in our lives; He wants to be involved in the most intimate of ways, through a relationship that revolves around faith and trust. In times of pressure and questioning when we seek His will, God has the intention of drawing us into a more intimate relationship with Him.

Think about a time when you had to make a big decision; you prayed diligently and finally came to a conclusion about God's plan. Not only did you arrive at an action plan, but you also emerged from the situation amazed at the goodness and grace of God. You had not only more information about what He wanted you to do, but also an awareness of who He is and how much He loves you.

God is involved in this process. And while we might simply want information, He wants us to trust Him. The principle of discovering God's will is couched in the context of a relationship. He is working to reveal Himself to you because He wants you to walk away from the process with your faith stronger and your relationship more intimate.

There is an island in the Bahamas called Inagua, and from that island they export salt. There is a harbor that has been dredged out and is large enough for big ships to dock and get the salt. The water is not very deep, so the ships' captains have to be careful once they come inside the reef to stay inside the channels.

I was photographing in the area and noticed a very interesting phenomenon. On the mainland behind the harbor was a large pole. About forty yards behind that one, farther inland, was another one. A third pole was positioned in alignment in the distance. I figured this had to do with the ships' navigation but wasn't sure how it worked. I asked a man standing nearby to explain their function. He said, "Well, those are channel markers."

I responded, "Channel markers are usually in the channel. These are on the island. So how does this work?"

"What happens is, as a ship approaches the island, the captain of the ship can see these three poles. He has to keep maneuvering his ship so that all three poles line up. And once they are aligned, he knows he is in the channel and can approach the island safely."

What God has done for us through His Word is give us channel markers that assure us when things are lined up, we know we are following His will.

I want you to be impressed with the incredible, practical approach God gives us to discern His will. It is not some kind of mysterious journey. He has given us objective channel markers to help us know whether or not our decisions agree with his will for our life.

The first channel marker is God's moral will. God will never lead you to do anything that is in conflict with His moral will. Any decision you make or any option you choose that conflicts with God's moral will is not of God. He will never *lead* a husband to leave his wife for a "more spiritual" woman. God will never *lead* a teenager to rebel against his or her parents. God will never *lead* you to cheat on your income tax in order to give more money to the church. God doesn't operate like that.

God's moral will plays another important role. Obeying His moral will, the things that are clear, is the foundation for decision-making in the more challenging arena of discerning His personal will. In John 14:21, Jesus puts it this way: "He who has My commandments and keeps them, it is he who loves Me. And he who loves Me will be loved by My Father, and I will love him and manifest Myself to him."

The man or woman who develops a lifestyle in harmony with God's moral commands will experience God's guidance in a special way. When you and I live lives of obedience, we are consistently in step with God's thought and God's ways. It makes sense that we are able to discern His voice more easily.

You are going to have a difficult time discerning God's personal will if you ignore His moral will. Why? Because God is not interested in simply being an information center. He is interested in an intimate relationship with you.

There is a second marker—the principles of God's Word. The difference between God's moral will and His principles is this: God's moral will is a set of clear commands. "This is what you do. This is what you don't do." His principles, however, are more like equations—an equation where God says, "If a man does this, he can expect this to happen. If a woman does this, she can expect this to happen."

A principle is the law of sowing and reaping. We always reap what we sow. Another principle: things that you hold tightly to diminish; things that you scatter and give are multiplied and returned. "There is one who scatters, yet increases more; and there is one who withholds more than is right, but it leads to poverty" (Prov. 11:24).

The Bible is full of principles. And here is the key: At some point in your decision-making, your options will intersect with the principles of God's Word. The Bible is so incredibly packed with principles, it is impossible to face any decision and not intersect with the principles of God's Word. They serve as a checks and balance system in the decision-making process.

Discovering the will of God is not the result of spending hours in a spiritual darkroom. God has made it far simpler than that. He gave us principles that coincide with all the choices we make. God wants to renew your mind with His principles.

Principles take precedent over a sense of inner peace. God does not want us to be slaves to vacillating feelings. He is far more practical than that. If you will keep God's moral will and constantly renew your mind to what is true, then, as the decisions come along, you will be able to sort out the options and discern that the will of God is for you. How practical. How wonderful.

Do you spend time in God's Word every day? If you don't and if you are not in some sort of systematic discipline to fill your mind with God's principles, you are going to have a difficult time making the right decisions, because the key to decision-making is the principles of His Word. Promises have a role, but they are girded by the principles.

There is a third marker—wisdom. Ephesians 5:15 says, "See then that you walk circumspectly, not as fools but as wise." God has called us to ask of every invitation, every opportunity, every business transaction, every family decision, this important question: Is this the wise thing to do?

This question will quickly reveal your motive. It will reveal the selfishness in your relationships. It will reveal the greed in your financial decisions. In light of my present state of mind, in light of what's going on at work, in light of what's going on in my life right now, is this the wise thing for me to do? In light of where I want to be in the future, in light of the kind of marriage and the kind of family I want to have, in light of where I want to be financially, in light of where I want to be in terms of my career, in light of where I want to be in terms of my ability to serve God, is this the wise thing to do?

So in decision-making, the place to start is measuring the decision against God's moral will. You have to measure it against the principles of His Word, and you have to measure it against whether it's a wise choice. If you do these things and still don't know God's mind, an example from Paul's missionary journeys is helpful.

Do you know how Paul decided which cities to visit? Paul apparently went where he wanted. He wasn't trapped by thinking, *Oh, what if I do the wrong thing? What if I step out of God's will?* He understood the incredible principle that God's will is not a tightrope that we fall from. Acts 16:7 gives insight: "After they had come to Mysia, they tried to go into Bithynia, but the Spirit did not permit them."

A key word is *tried*. They tried to go to Bithynia. It is where they wanted to go. We don't know how, but somehow Jesus said, "Paul, this isn't the right route."

Paul, in his own way, said, "OK, no problem." He did not get depressed or discouraged; he just started out in a new direction. God, through His Word, has demonstrated that if children of God are willing to be honest and, to the best of their ability, do what God wants them to do, He will intervene if they make faulty decisions and point us in a new direction.

Excerpted from *The Glorious Journey* by Charles Stanley (Nashville: Thomas Nelson, Inc., 1996), 227–231. Used by permission.

If any of you lacks wisdom, let him ask of God, who gives to all liberally and without reproach, and it will be given

Y2J Yield to Jesus

to him. But let him ask in faith, with no doubting, for he who doubts is like a wave of the sea driven and tossed by the wind. For let not that man suppose that he will receive anything from the Lord; he is a double-minded man, unstable in all his ways. (James 1:5–8)

READER'S NOTES:

_____

_____

_____

_____

_____

_____

Are You a Disciple?

━━━━━━━━━━━━━━━━━━━━━━━━━━━━━

How we learn, is what we learn.

—Bonnie Friedman (1958 –)
Writing Past Dark

BY CHARLES STANLEY

Jesus stated that we are called beyond simply enjoying the benefits and blessings of salvation; we are to be disciples of Christ. Coming to terms with what a disciple is and what is involved keeps many Christians from pursuing this call. When they start hearing words like *deny* and *sacrifice*, they opt out of the discipling process.

Defining how a disciple must live causes us to hold hands up in protest and say, "Hey, wait a minute! This is starting to sound like a lot more than I bargained for! It's starting to sound like I've got to sacrifice something." And that's exactly what Jesus was saying. Becoming a child of God will cost you nothing because it cost Christ everything. However, becoming a disciple of Jesus Christ could possibly cost a great deal.

The part about denying ourselves and sacrifice bothers Christians today, as it did the disciples. What exactly does that mean? Being a disciple—or follower—of Christ is essentially this: when your desire and God's desire are in conflict, you go with what God wants. When Christ asks for A and you want B, you do A in obedience to Him. Being a follower of Christ is not just believing in something, it's about wrestling daily with this statement: "Here's what I want; here's what God wants. To be a follower of Christ, I have to choose what God wants over what I want."

The idea of having to deny ourselves is one thing, but the notion of losing life if we try to "save it" and saving it if we "lose it" for Christ is confusing, at best. Jesus' teaching means that when we say no to Him because we're afraid of missing out on life, we will most certainly miss out on life! Jesus knew that life is not found in the things we think—job, money, material possessions—it is found in God alone.

Until your purpose lines up with God's purpose, you will never be happy or fulfilled. Christ said that He came that you might have life and have it more abundantly. The only way you can experience abundant life is to surrender your plans to Him.

God's purpose is that we *be* disciples and then *make* disciples. By saying no to ourselves, we are allowing God the opportunity to fulfill in us His purpose. It is a choice that every believer must make sooner or later. Everyone who accepts Jesus' death at Calvary as the sufficient payment for sins will go to heaven. Discipleship has nothing to do with whether you will go to heaven or not. It has everything to do with whether you will find authentic purpose in life.

Jesus declared that we are to "go therefore and make disciples" (Matt. 28:19). However, before we can make disciples, we must be disciples. With this instruction, the next step is to determine what a disciple is and then choose whether we will answer the call. It is possible to be a child of God and never be a disciple of Christ. We can live the Christian life with the assurance of heaven as our ultimate destiny but still miss the process of maturing as a disciple.

Nothing worth having is obtained without a price. Being a disciple involves becoming a learner, a student of the Master. That means studying His Word, participating in Bible study, absorbing everything you can through the teaching ministry of your church. It means developing an ongoing relationship with Jesus through prayer and study. A disciple is a learner. You must learn about the One you are to follow and equip yourself for the work He will direct you to do.

A disciple is a follower of Christ. That means you take on His priorities as your own. His agenda becomes your agenda. His mission becomes your mission.

We should be involved in and concerned about many worthy causes, but if all we do is make people more comfortable and feel better about themselves, we miss the heartbeat of discipleship. A disciple of Christ understands that the priority is to impact the *outcome* of people's journey. That was Christ's mission. This is what He has called us to do as well.

Excerpted from *The Glorious Journey* by Charles Stanley (Nashville: Thomas Nelson, Inc., 1996), 460–461. Used by permission.

When He had called the people to Himself, with His disciples also, He said to them, "Whoever desires to come after Me, let him deny himself, and take up his

cross, and follow Me. For whoever desires to save his life will lose it, but whoever loses his life for My sake and the gospel's will save it. For what will it profit a man if he gains the whole world, and loses his own soul? Or what will a man give in exchange for his soul? For whoever is ashamed of Me and My words in this adulterous and sinful generation, of him the Son of Man also will be ashamed when He comes in the glory of His Father with the holy angels." (Mark 8:34–38)

READER'S NOTES:

_____

_____

_____

_____

_____

_____

CONSECRATED TO HIM

It must be a prospect pleasing to God to see his creatures forever drawing nearer to him by greater degrees of resemblance.

—Joseph Addison (1672–1719)
English essayist

BY TERRY MEEUWSEN

M ost of us would be moderately uncomfortable with the thought that we could be holy. Holiness seems to be an attribute reserved for God, but beyond that a lot of us would have a difficult time trying to verbalize exactly what it is. Yet way back in the book of Leviticus, God clearly says to His people, "Be holy, for I am the Lord your God" (Lev. 20:7).

It is almost impossible for me to comprehend God's Holiness. His holiness is the antithesis of what I am and what I know, and it evokes all kinds of feelings in me—from sheer terror to trembling reverence.

I have been reading numerous Scripture passages and books on the holiness of God, and my reading has caused me to reflect on how cavalierly we treat God in the midst of such incredible blessings.

As I was running an errand yesterday, I looked at the scenes passing by my car window. Beautiful homes with lovely yards; people golfing in designer clothing on perfectly manicured fairways; stores stocked with everything we could desire; lakes and trees and wildlife; people fishing and swimming and biking. In the midst of it all, I was struck with how much we are given and how much we take for granted. I was overwhelmed with how much God has provided for us. And I was overwhelmed with how seldom we acknowledged Him for it.

This biblical warning came to mind: "Beware that you do not forget the Lord your God . . . lest when you have eaten and are full, and have built beautiful houses and dwell in them; and when your herds and your flocks multiply, and your silver and your gold are multiplied, and all that you have is multiplied; when your heart is lifted up, and you forget the Lord your God" (Deut. 8:11–14). Words we need to heed.

When we glimpse the greatness of our God, we often want to do something to honor him. We are like Peter when he saw Jesus in His glory with Moses and Elijah. He said, "If You wish, let us make here three tabernacles" (Matt. 17:4).

But in the book of Micah, God tells us what He requires of us to be pleasing to Him. "With what shall I come before the Lord, / And bow myself before the High God? / Shall I come before Him with burnt offerings, / With calves a year old? / Will the Lord be pleased with thousands of rams, / Ten thousand rivers of oil? / Shall

I give my firstborn for my transgression, / The fruit of my body for the sin of my soul? / He has shown you, O man, what is good; / And what does the Lord require of you / But to do justly, / To love mercy, / And to walk humbly with your God?" (Mic. 6:6–8).

God isn't looking for perfect men and women; God isn't asking us to build great monuments to Him. God is looking for people who will reverence Him in their hearts and in their lifestyles. God is looking for people in whom He can take up residence, with whom He can speak and walk, through whom He can work. He is looking for people who are willing to be set apart.

> Lord, I know that You understand my shortcomings, for You created me. But I also know that You are holy and awesome and that Your purposes for Your people far exceed what I could dream or imagine. Forgive me for being distracted from You. I bow my heart and my knee to You, the King of kings and Lord of lords. Perform a work in me that I might be pleasing in Your sight, O God. My heart cries out with Your angels as they call to one another, "Holy, Holy, Holy is the Lord of hosts; / The whole earth is full of His glory!" (Isa. 6:3).

Excerpted from *Near to the Heart of God* by Terry Meeuwsen (Nashville: Thomas Nelson, Inc., 1998), 236–239. Used by permission.

For it pleased the Father that in Him all the fullness should dwell, and by Him to reconcile all things to Himself, by Him, whether things on earth or things in heaven, having made peace through the blood of His

cross. And you, who once were alienated and enemies in your mind by wicked works, yet now He has reconciled in the body of His flesh through death, to present you holy, and blameless, and above reproach in His sight. (Col. 1:19–23)

READER'S NOTES:

_____

_____

_____

_____

_____

_____

GOD SPEAKS THROUGH
THE LIFE OF JESUS

The Lord Jesus is the Holiest among the mighty, and the Mightiest among the holy, who has lifted with His pierced hands empires off their hinges, turned the stream of centuries out of its channel, and still governs the ages.

—Jean Paul Richter (1763–1825)
German novelist

BY BECKY TIRABASSI

The Bible clearly has a central and most controversial focus: Jesus. In the Old Testament, Jesus is concealed, but foretold as the Son of God who would come to earth as the Messiah. In the New Testament, He is revealed, rules, and reigns as God's only means of reconciliation with man. Therefore, the Bible speaks to every generation who came before and after Jesus Christ about the opportunity to be in a relationship with God, the Father and Creator.

Blaise Pascal, the great French mathematician and physicist in the 1600s was one of the most influential men to explain to the skeptics of his time the dynamic opportunity a person has to communicate with God. Boldly, he discussed his beliefs in the *Pensées:*

We know God only through Jesus Christ. Without this mediator, all communication with God is broken off. Through Jesus we know God. All those who have claimed to know God and prove his existence without Jesus Christ have only had futile proofs to offer. But to prove Christ, we have the prophecies which are solid and palpable proofs. By being fulfilled and proved true by the event, these prophecies show that these truths are certain and thus prove that Jesus is divine. In him and through him, therefore, we know God. Apart from that, without Scripture, without original sin, without the necessary mediator, who was promised and came, it is impossible to prove absolutely that God exists, or to teach sound doctrine and sound morality. But through and in Christ we can prove God's existence, and teach both doctrine and morality. Therefore Jesus is the true God of men.

In Pascal's mind, it was "not only impossible, but useless to know God without Christ." He believed God was attainable to those who acknowledged that the Son, Jesus Christ, was God in human form.

Pascal spoke to the scholar and to the uneducated alike, arguing that to know God is not unreachable for anyone, but attainable by anyone who acknowledges the person of Jesus Christ was God in time and history. Jesus was called the living, incarnate Word. We can know of Him by reading about Him in the Word. We can know Him personally by entering into a relationship with Him by faith!

Excerpted from *Let Faith Change Your Life* by Becky Tirabassi (Nashville: Thomas Nelson, Inc.,1997), 71–73. Used by permission.

> **In the beginning was the Word, and the Word was with God, and the Word was God. He was in the beginning with God. All things were made through Him, and without Him nothing was made that was made. In Him was life, and the life was the light of men. And the light shines in the darkness, and the darkness did not comprehend it. (John 1:1–5)**

READER'S NOTES:

_____

_____

_____

_____

_____

_____

Radical Faith

██

> Faith is the highest passion in a human being. Many in
> every generation may not come that far, but none comes
> further.
>
> —Soren Kierkegaard (1813–1855)
> Danish philosopher

BY BECKY TIRABASSI

I find it astonishing that the Ten Commandments have been taken out of the classrooms of American public schools, but they are being added to the former Soviet Union classrooms! I am utterly amazed that our nation does *not* want to promote the Judeo-Christian morals, yet a nation (formerly the USSR) subjected to seventy-three years of godlessness and communism is desperately seeking moral teaching for its students!

What does this reaction imply about our country? How can Americans be so afraid of time-proven guidelines for moral living?

Perhaps it is too threatening to a society that is heralded for its liberal ideals and laziness toward duty, respect, honesty, and purity to be asked to consider morality as an esteemed goal? Perhaps words such as *honor* and *sacrifice* have become too demanding? Maybe today's leaders no longer want to push, or be pushed, toward higher standards? These are questions a moral code answers for men, women, and country.

C. S. Lewis, whom *Time* magazine described as "one of the most influential spokesmen for Christianity in the English-speaking world," once said, "Morals are directions for running the human machine." The Bible clearly states that there are physical, spiritual, *and* moral laws in the universe. It goes as far as to give the details of its origination—the places, times, and people to whom these laws were given. And they were clearly and specifically not man-made laws, but laws based upon and derived from the very character of God. Yes, they were called "commands." And from before the beginning of recorded time, these commands—God's commands—contained absolutes that defined right from wrong as well as differentiated good from evil.

Hence, it logically follows that if someone chooses to violate, ignore, or break any of those commands or absolutes, he or she is really choosing to rebel against God. It also follows that those who rebel against Him expose themselves to predetermined consequences that will inevitably lead to personal moral breakdown. Parents know this pattern as "breaking the rules" and "suffering the consequences," though not all parents can uphold their rules or handle the rebellion of their children! God defines this rebellion as sin, which sadly results in separation between man and God, or man and others.

Have you noticed how the word *sin* raises the tone and temperature of a conversation when it is discussed? Why is *sin* such a harsh and threatening word in our culture? And why is it considered too presumptuous of a holy God to give standards, design rules, or set boundaries that have predetermined consequences attached to them? Perhaps the true question is, "Could all men and women live in peace and harmony without a written moral code to guide them?"

Throughout history, we proved that we are not pure enough in motive or character to be each other's peacemakers, authoritarians, or judges. Our perception is limited and finite, our motives are skewed selfishly, and our track record over time speaks for itself! Only the Bible, because it is based on the character and absolutes of a holy God, is able to purely and justly give moral standards and answers to men and women by which to live.

If the Bible is considered true in teaching and precept for every generation, it would follow that it should elicit a response from those who read it. As a society, many Americans have opted to ignore and even ridicule the unchanging morals and values of their Judeo-Christian heritage found in the Bible. Instead of referring to the Ten Commandments or the Golden Rule (which only up until forty years ago were posted in most American public school classrooms) as truth by which all people might live, we have resorted to judging life by the standards of values that each individual has deemed personally significant or satisfying. Needless to say, even without detailed documentation, I believe that our nation has approached such moral decay that kids killing kids and carrying guns is the "norm" rather than an appalling, unacceptable way of life. Without respect for the teaching in the Bible, we have become a nation where lust and selfishness have replaced goodness and love.

I don't need to judge this observation by anyone else's life. I only need to look as far as my own life to be certain that not a lack of, but a rejection of, moral teaching was the cause of my demise. By letting self-fulfillment drive my life, I immediately gauged all my decisions and choices by what *felt* good to me rather than a code of ethics centered in truth and morality.

I actually remember living off the self-talk popular in the seventies that continually reminded me that only *I* mattered. Within a few short years, the results of the self-counsel proved to completely bankrupt me physically, mentally, financially, and emotionally.

Then to what do I attribute my revised change in attitude, action, and focus? It was not a guru, an organization, or another popular seventies cure—a mantra. With great sincerity, I am personally convinced that I would not be free of drugs and alcohol, married, and deeply committed to one man for nineteen years, the parent of a great young man, *or even alive* had I not let the moral teachings of the Bible influence my life for the last twenty years. I believe that the time-tested set of moral laws that I was taught as a child, but only as an adult determined to live by, is the teaching that changed my life in 1976 and afforded me a wonderful quality of life ever since.

Excerpted from *Let Faith Change Your Life* by Becky Tirabassi (Nashville: Thomas Nelson, Inc.,1997), 93–96. Used by permission.

And God spoke all these words saying;
"I am the Lord your God, who brought you out of the

land of Egypt, out of the house of bondage.

"You shall have no other gods before Me.

"You shall not make for yourself a carved image—any likeness of anything that is in heaven above, or that is in the earth beneath, or that is in the water under the earth; you shall not bow down to them nor serve them. For I, the Lord your God, am a jealous God, visiting the iniquity of the fathers upon the children to the third and fourth generations of those who hate Me, but showing mercy to thousands, to those who love Me and keep My commandments.

"You shall not take the name of the Lord your God in vain, for the Lord will not hold him guiltless who takes His name in vain.

"Remember the Sabbath day, to keep it holy. Six days you shall labor and do all your work, but the seventh day is the Sabbath of the Lord your God. In it you shall do no work; you, nor your son, nor your daughter, nor your male servant, nor your female servant, nor your cattle, nor your stranger who is within your gates. For in six days the Lord made the heavens and the earth, the sea, and all that is in them, and rested the seventh day. Therefore the Lord blessed the Sabbath day and hallowed it.

"Honor your father and your mother, that your days may be long upon the land which the Lord your God is giving you.

"You shall not murder.

"You shall not commit adultery.

"You shall not steal.

"You shall not bear false witness against your neighbor.

"You shall shall not covet your neighbor's house; you shall not covet your neighbor's wife, nor his male servant, nor his female servant, nor his ox, nor his donkey, nor anything that is your neighbor's." (Ex. 20:1–17)

READER'S NOTES:

_____

_____

_____

_____

_____

_____

SOME ASSEMBLY REQUIRED

God has placed no limits to the exercise of the intellect He
has given us, on this side of the grave.

—Francis Bacon (1561–1626)
English journalist, scientist, author, and philosopher

Three of the scariest words in the English language are *ready to
assemble*. I doubt there is a parent anywhere who hasn't assembled a
child's toy without finding leftover parts lying around. Not only that,
when reviewing the instructions, most parents find they are clueless as
to where the spare parts belong. Think of all the leftover parts that have
ended up in landfills along with the Christmas tree. How many toys
have performed "not quite right" because they had to be assembled?

What if we didn't have any instructions? My husband, Boo, is big
about ignoring instructions. I am sure many of you reading this story
can relate. He thinks that since he knows what the finished product

looks like, it should be simple to figure out where all the parts go. You would think he would have learned his lesson twenty-five years ago when he started our Christian gift manufacturing business.

While sitting in a courtroom several years ago, Boo noticed a carved walnut name sign on the judge's desk. The thought ran through his mind, *I could sell a lot of those.*

When leaving the courtroom, he "approached the bench" and got the manufacturer's name off the desk sign. When he contacted the "manufacturer," he discovered it wasn't a big company at all, but a retired colonel who carved these signs in his garage to supplement his income. Located only a couple of hundred miles from our home, the colonel said yes to Boo's visitation of the manufacturing "operation."

The colonel graciously listened to Boo's enthusiastic proposal to sell his product, but in the end, he told Boo, he really didn't need any more business. The income he made through word of mouth was sufficient for his needs. All of Boo's sales instincts could not convince him otherwise. Yet, before Boo left the colonel, another option occurred to him. *What if he could make these desk name signs himself?*

Can you imagine what went through the mind of this kindly old colonel? He probably didn't feel Boo was any threat to his business, since Boo had never operated any of the machines used to make the signs. The extent of Boo's woodshop experience was a hammer, nails, and occasionally a paintbrush.

Nevertheless, Boo and the colonel decided on a day when Boo could come watch the process, start to finish. A few days later, Boo returned to our apartment with a list of machines and his own "how-to" list in hand. With the meager amount of cash we had left to our name, Boo bought every piece of equipment he was told he needed.

He assumed that once he had everything he needed, the rest would just work itself out.

I asked Boo, "Do you know how to use all this stuff?"

He replied rather indignantly, "I watched the colonel." *OK,* I thought, *this ought to be good.* To this day I still marvel at the miracle that transpired in that garage for Boo's business to become the company it is today.

When Boo turned on the first machine to begin, the most *critical* machine for the process, the saw blade broke. Since Boo only purchased one blade the first time, you can understand he didn't catch on very easily; he broke at least eleven blades that first day before he sought help!

My attempts at assembly and instructions weren't much better; I should've been given a manual when I left the hospital with my newborns. Both my children were born with all their parts, but that is not who they are! In part, who they are is a result of having parents who purposed to live a yielded life in Christ. Yes, there were times when the "assembly" didn't go as planned. There were many days of "broken blades," but help in instruction was always available through God's Word.

> For I know the thoughts that I think toward you, says the LORD, thoughts of peace and not of evil, to give you a future and a hope. Then you will call upon Me and go and pray to Me, and I will listen to you. And you will seek Me and find Me, when you search for Me with all your heart. (Jer. 29:11–13)

READER'S NOTES:

THE EVENING NEWS

The new electronic interdependence recreates the world
in the image of a global village.

—Marshall McLuhan (1911–1980)
Canadian communications theorist

I *f it bleeds, it leads.* On April 20, 1999, Columbine High School
in Littleton, Colorado, was the scene of a bloody rampage. Two
students carrying guns and wearing trench coats left fifteen dead—
fourteen students (including the killers) and one teacher. In recent
years several schools across America have been victims of kids
wielding guns. The last shooting involving the greatest loss of lives
occurred on March 24, 1998, in Jonesboro, Arkansas.

As I write this, it is the fourth day of televised updates of the
Littleton aftermath and details of the victims' and shooters' lives.
Those who make their living on the news have a lot on their plate

this week, choosing between calamity at home and the crisis in Kosovo: if it bleeds, it leads.

But I want to point out something that our broadcasting friends seem to gloss over or ignore. Perhaps I have missed a lone broadcaster pointing this out and if so, I apologize, but I have seen a most obvious telling detail that any viewer with a remote control could find. I can flip to any station on the television and I will hear the words *prayer* or *God* and find people gathered in churches for prayer vigils and kneeling in prayer at temporary memorials in Littleton and in Kosovo, where innocent victims pray to survive the crisis.

Two nights after the tragedy in Littleton, Ted Koppell, host of *Nightline,* held a town meeting between the Jonesboro, Arkansas survivors and some of the Littleton, Colorado children and adults. Their premise was to some way help Littleton with dialogue between the two cities. It was glaringly obvious to me as I watched that the grief in Jonesboro is still very fresh. However, they encouraged reaching out to each other and praying about it.

In fact, one of the teachers at Columbine High School was credited by her students for having kept them calm by praying during the four hours they were held hostage.

When a Burlington, Wisconsin high school principal was interviewed about his school avoiding similar terror and loss because of an informant, his primary statement was, "The Lord was with us that day." The broadcaster did not pursue that comment.

If it bleeds, it leads. We are becoming experts at grief. In their defense, it is the newscasters' job to report the story, but more often than not "the rest of the story" remains untold: people coming to Christ through a tragic loss, broken relationships healed by turning to each other and to the Lord, lives once apathetic to Christ becoming more significant when what truly matters becomes evident.

The crisis in America is not kids with guns, single-parent families, welfare, or corruption in government or men at war. The crisis is America is the absence of the Lord in people's lives, homes, workplace, schools, and places of authority.

Imagine, if you will, what would happen if every newscaster took a comment about God or prayer or acknowledged churches as places of change, refuge and healing and gave equal time to these comments like they do with tragic stories. And what if news magazine interviewers, when hearing the request, "Pray for us," responded with the words, "Let's just pray right now"? Think about it.

> **For I am not ashamed of the gospel of Christ, for it is the power of God to salvation for everyone who believes, for the Jew first and also for the Greek. For in it the righteousness of God is revealed from faith to faith; as it is written, "The just shall live by faith." (Rom. 1:16–17)**

READER'S NOTES:

_____

_____

_____

_____

_____

_____

ASTHMA AT 13,000 FEET

To yield means to trust that the One you are trusting can accomplish it just as well as or better than you.

—Boo Courrege (1948–)

When our children were in high school, my husband, Boo, and I would go along on ski trips as resident "Mom and Pop" chaperones. We really didn't have a defined job description other than being "visible" surrogate parents just in case the kids needed a parent, which was rare. We prepared the evening meals for 50 après skiers, sat in during their fellowship time, and sometimes we even got to ski!

One evening one of our young friends, Carrie, had difficulty breathing. Though having trouble breathing at high altitudes is not uncommon, this had never happened to Carrie before, so it warranted our attention.

My husband and I are not strangers to asthma. He and both my children carry ventolin inhalers for those times when their breathing is so constricted that they need help to open their air passages. Carrie's symptoms had all the earmarks of an asthma attack.

A handful of inhalers were available; we decided to give Carrie the common dosage to see if it helped her breathing. She did get immediate relief but soon after, her symptoms returned and we knew she needed medical attention.

It was late at night in Breckenridge, Colorado, and more than the slopes were closed—all the medical facilities were shut down. We found an emergency room twenty miles away and that was our only option.

It never occurred to my husband that any other person should take Carrie other than himself. We had made plenty of these emergency runs with our own children. Boo held his keys and Carrie close at hand, and together with her older brother and the wife of our youth pastor, they took off.

Carrie's parents are two of our closest friends. I knew how they would feel when I called them to tell them Carrie was on her way to the hospital. The next hour or so was filled with prayer from Carrie's parents, our entire youth group, and the chaperones. Hearts were heavy until we received word that yes, Carrie had experienced an acute asthma attack and would be fine as soon as she completed the prescribed treatment at the hospital.

Carrie's parents kept in contact with us, and they were relieved to learn the good news. Later, Boo told me that Carrie's dad, Don, said that even though Carrie was 500 miles away, he was comforted by the fact that Carrie was with Boo and he trusted him to take care of her.

This is what yielding is all about. My husband describes it this way, "To yield means to trust that the one you are trusting can accomplish it as well as or better than you."

Carrie's parents yielded the responsibility to handle the crisis to Boo because it was out of their control. Do you see the same parallel in yielding to God? Yielding in all things. We should trust God, Jesus, and the Holy Spirit to take care of all things in a manner far superior to anything we can do in our own strength. Yield to the One whose perfect will has only the best for us on His mind. All things considered, why would I choose otherwise?

> Now He who searches the hearts knows what the mind of the Spirit is, because He makes intercession for the saints according to the will of God. And we know that all things work together for good to those who love God, to those who are called according to His purpose. (Rom. 8:27–28)

READER'S NOTES:

_____

_____

_____

_____

_____

_____

CALL FOR REPENTANCE

We have been the recipients of the choicest bounties of heaven. We have been preserved, these many years, in peace and prosperity. We have grown in numbers, wealth, and power as no other nation has ever grown. But we have forgotten God. We have forgotten the gracious hand which preserved us in peace, and multiplied and enriched and strengthened us; and we have vainly imagined, in the deceitfulness of our hearts, that all these blessings were produced by some superior wisdom and virtue of our own. Intoxicated with unbroken success, we have become too self-sufficient to feel the necessity of redeeming and preserving grace, too proud to pray to the God that made us! It behooves us, then, to humble ourselves before the offended Power, to confess our national sins, and to pray for clemency and forgiveness.

—Abraham Lincoln

Proclamation for a National Day of Fasting,
Humiliation and Prayer, April 30, 1863

Since 1988 America has recognized the first Thursday in May as an official day of prayer. That is a good beginning, but is it enough?

The Bible lists many instances of what can happen when a country is repentant and when a country is not.

Ninevah was considered a great city. Founded by Noah's great-grandson, Nimrod, it was the capital of the Assyrian Empire. At the height of its prosperity, it had a population of 120,000. It would take an entire day for a traveler to journey to the center of the city from its outskirts. The Ninevites enjoyed the best chariots, fine food and entertainment, and incredible wealth of industry for their time.

Sadly, the Assyrian kings were cruel and ruthless. Their armies invaded and pillaged the homeland of the Israelites over and over again. When the prophet Jonah visited the city, he wanted God to destroy this pagan nation. After all, that was what they deserved. Jonah 3:10 tells us that although Jonah felt the city deserved to be destroyed for its wickedness, the nation repented and was spared by a compassionate and merciful God.

However, moving forward to the book of Nahum, we find that Ninevah was eventually destroyed 150 years later by their enemies. Ninevah received the grace period because of the families who repented, but they fell back into their immorality, corruption, and lives of luxury. Nahum 2:3–3:7 describes the city's ungodliness and final destruction—so devastating that it remained hidden until 1840.

Every age has considered itself to be superior to preceding times; yet, Lincoln's speech is still relevant today. It would have been relevant for Ninevah. Progress has brought about even greater change in morality than it has in technology. A change in morality is sin, not progress. If God is comparing the sin of Ninevah to the sin that is so prevalent in the world today, do you wonder if we are in our grace period?

> Then the LORD appeared to Solomon by night, and said to him: "I have heard your prayer, and have chosen this place for Myself as a house of sacrifice. When I shut up heaven and there is no rain, or command the locusts to devour the land, or send pestilence among My people, if My people who are called by My name will humble themselves, and pray and seek My face, and turn from their wicked ways, then I will hear from heaven, and will forgive their sin and heal their land. Now My eyes will be open and My ears attentive to prayer made in this place." (2 Chron. 7:12–15)

READER'S NOTES:

_____
_____
_____
_____
_____
_____

WHAT ABOUT VERSES FOR WHEN YOU'RE HAPPY?

Happiness is neither within us only, or without us; it is
the union of ourselves with God.

—Blaise Pascal (1623–62)
French mathematician and philosopher

Our 25-year-old son, Cord, affectionately known as the web-
master, was building our company's Web site and wanted to have a
Bible verse on our page that would change every day. I gave him a
book of Bible promises that has verses isolated by category. After a few
minutes perusing the book, Cord exclaimed, "Mom! These headings
are for when you are about to eat a revolver, jump off a bridge, or
wrap a piano wire around your neck. What about verses for when
you're happy?"

Cord has a way with words, but when I considered what he really
meant, I saw his point.

Why is it we seem to isolate verses during times of crisis? Why do we tend to wait until we are at the end of our rope, so to speak, to seek the Lord? Of course, there is comfort in the Scriptures. But there are times when life isn't all panic. What about those verses for when we are happy?

Seeking is yielding, and when we're happy, we're seeking. We should be seeking God all the time. Yielding is turning to God for the little things and the big things, during the good times and the bad.

We grow too comfortable, confident, and complacent when things are good. These traits have other connotations, though.

1. Comfortable—*content*

2. Confident—*sure of oneself*

3. Complacent—*smug*

I agree, there is nothing wrong with being comfortable. And in the right context, confidence is okay. But if we become too content or sure of ourselves, then wouldn't smugness tend to creep in?

Cord had a good point. We need to seek those verses for when we are happy so we do not lose sight of who is the giver of that happiness. When I think about life's ups and downs, twisting and turning, I find that during the smooth times I don't seek God as earnestly as I certainly do when things are not going well.

Let me challenge you as well as myself to find those Scriptures for happiness, satisfaction, blessedness, contentment, joy, delight, gladness, enrichment, and cheerfulness. I'll help get us started:

Whom have I in heaven but You?
And there is none upon earth that I desire besides You.
My flesh and my heart fail,
But God is the strength of my heart and my portion
forever. (Ps. 73:25–26)

READER'S NOTES:

_____

_____

_____

_____

_____

_____

THE BIBLE SAYS . . .

I speak as a man of the world, to men of the world; and I
say to you, Search the Scriptures! The Bible is the book of
all others, to be read at all ages, and in all conditions of
human life; not to be read once or twice or thrice through,
and then laid aside, but to be read in small portions of one
or two chapters every day, and never to be intermitted,
unless by some overruling necessity.

—John Quincy Adams (1767–1848)
Sixth U.S. President

Thirty-five years ago I was saved at a Billy Graham crusade. As
a follow-up to his crusade, employees of Billy Graham's organization
sent packets of Bible verses to "baby" Christians to help them in their
new walk with Christ.

Through the years I've watched countless Graham crusades on television, and I cannot begin to tell you the times the words *The Bible says* have been spoken by Mr. Graham. What the Bible says should be the passion for every believer who wants to live a yielded life.

The Bible is the A-Z reference for everything! Sometimes when I am speaking to a group I say, "This is my opinion, and you're entitled to that opinion, since I am the one speaking." It usually gets my intended response, laughter. My audience should laugh. It is, after all, only *my opinion*.

If I chose to speak about Christian living and did not give several examples of what the Bible says, then, in my opinion, the words from my mouth would have little worth for my listeners.

Living a yielded life is impossible if we do not know what the Bible says. If I never knew with certainty what the Bible says, then my Christian walk would toss like the ocean's waves from one man's opinion to another.

What if I only sought advice from others around me when I needed to make a decision, when I found myself in a crisis, or when I needed to know right from wrong? If I never sought the Bible when my spirit was being compelled, how would I know what was compelling me? I would be hard-pressed to have any discernment.

Search the Scriptures. Read, meditate, and memorize their words. Know what the Bible says for everything in your life, from A-Z. In my opinion, a yielded life is yielding with trust and faith to what the Bible says, and I must search it every day.

All scripture is given by inspiration of God, and is profitable for doctrine, for reproof, for correction, for instruction in righteousness, that the man of God may be complete, thoroughly equipped for every good work. (2 Tim. 3:16–17)

READER'S NOTES:

_____

_____

_____

_____

_____

_____

_____

MISS AMY WHITTINGTON IS A DIFFERENCE MAKER

The miracle, or the power, that elevates the few is to be
found in their industry, application, and perseverance
under the promptings of a brave, determined spirit.
—Mark Twain [Samuel Clemens] (1835–1910)
American humorist

BY ZIG ZIGLAR

In our lifetime, each one of us influences both by word and by
deed—either for good or for bad—countless numbers of people.
That means all of us are difference makers.

Miss Amy Whittington would certainly qualify as one who
directly and indirectly influenced thousands of people. At age eighty-
three, she was still teaching a Sunday school class in Sault Sainte
Marie, Michigan. She learned that the Moody Bible Institute in
Chicago was offering a seminar to teach people how to be more

173

effective teachers. She literally saved her pennies until she had the necessary money to buy a bus ticket to Chicago. She rode the bus all night to attend the seminar to learn new methods and procedures so she could do a better job.

One of the professors, impressed with her age, enthusiasm, and the fact that she had ridden the bus all night to attend the seminar, engaged her in conversation. He asked her what age group she taught and how many were in her class. When she responded that she taught a class of junior high school boys and there were thirteen in the class, the professor asked how many kids belonged to the church. Miss Whittington replied, "Fifty." The professor, astonished that she taught more than 25 percent of the church youth, responded, "With that kind of record we should have you teach us how to teach." How right he was!

I hasten to add that people who are already good at what they do are far more likely to work at getting better than are those who are marginal performers. What kind of impact did Miss Amy Whittington have? Eighty-six of those boys she taught in her Sunday school class through the years ended up in the ministry. Can't you just imagine the thousands of people she directly and indirectly affected for good? She truly was a difference maker. You are, too, so make it a good difference.

Excerpted from *Something to Smile About*, by Zig Ziglar (Nashville: Thomas Nelson, Inc., 1997), 47–48. Used by permission.

I beseech you therefore, brethren, by the mercies of God, that you present your bodies a living sacrifice,

holy, acceptable to God, which is your reasonable
service. And do not be conformed to this world, but be
transformed by the renewing of your mind, that you
may prove what is that good and acceptable and perfect will of God. (Rom. 12:1–2)

READER'S NOTES:

_____

_____

_____

_____

_____

_____

COLUMBINE, FRIEND OF MINE

███

Assuredly, I say to you, wherever this gospel is preached
in the whole world, what this woman has done will also be
told as a memorial to her.

—Jesus

Matthew 26:13 (NKJV)

"Peace will come to you in time, Columbine, friend of mine . . ."

These words from a memorial song written by two brothers
from Columbine High School in Littleton, Colorado, are words of
hope for everyone left behind.

I watched the Columbine memorial service on April 22, 1999,
from my living room in Dallas, Texas. I was alone at home that
Sunday afternoon. Even though thousands of viewers were tuned in

to this fragile moment in tribute to students Cassie, Steven, Corey, Matt, Kyle, Rachel, Isaiah, John, Lauren, Daniel, and Kelly and teacher William Sanders, I felt God's comforting presence in every word, song, and action during the service as if every word was for me alone. I pray that the more than forty thousand people who attended the service felt the same.

Two days before Cassie Bernall stood face to face with her assassin and boldly professed, "Yes, I believe in God," she wrote a poem. One newspaper account says her brother found it the night of her death.

Here is part of her poem:

So, whatever it takes,
I will be the one who lives in the fresh
Newness of life of those who are
Alive from the dead.

Cassie's assurance that she indeed believed in God shows boldness and courage that every Christian would hope to have if he or she were asked the same question at gunpoint. Cassie was living a life yielded to her Lord. Are you living a yielded life? Could you say, "Yes, I believe!" to your accuser? Would you?

During the memorial service, beautiful white doves were released as the name of each student and the teacher was read in a final "roll call" on earth. For me that was a picture of the phrase from Cassie's poem, "fresh newness of life . . . alive from the dead." Each dove ascended toward heaven and the Lord in whose presence the "Cassies" of Columbine will reside forever.

Then He who sat on the throne said, "Behold I make all things new." And He said to me, "Write, for these words are true and faithful." And He said to me, "It is done! I am the Alpha and the Omega, the Beginning and the End. I will give of the fountain of the water of life freely to him who thirsts. He who overcomes shall inherit all things, and I will be his God and he shall be My son." (Rev. 21:5–7)

READER'S NOTES:

_____

_____

_____

_____

_____

_____

NOTES

1. Tim Hansel, *Through the Wilderness of Loneliness* (Colorado Springs: Chariot/Victor Publishing, 1991).

2. Dr. Edward Pauley, *Footsteps to Follow* (Nashville: J. Countryman/ Word Publishing Division of Thomas Nelson, Inc., 1998), 171.

3. Lewis Carroll, a conversation of Alice and the White Queen in *Through the Looking-Glass*, "Wool and Water" (1872)

4. From "In the Garden," words by C. Austin Miles (1868–1946).

5. From "Turn Your Eyes upon Jesus," words by Helen H. Lemmel (1864-1961).

6. Electronically retrieved from <http://members.truepath.com/ PathLightDevotionals/JWprayerB.htm>; Internet (23 January 1996).